FUTURE OF PAKISTAN

From Fear to Faith · From Power to People

BUTTERFLYMAN

A Vision of Faith, Justice, and Human Dignity

إنَّ اللَّهَ لَا يُغَيِّرُ مَا بِقَوْمٍ حَتَّى يُغَيِّرُوا مَا بِأَنْفُسِهِمْ

For permission requests, contact:
ButterflyMan Publishing LLC
Email: contact@butterflyman.com
Website: www.ButterflyMan.com

This book is a work of nonfiction.
All interpretations, analyses, and viewpoints are the author's own.

First Edition — 2025
Printed in the United States of America

ISBN: 979-8-90217-003-7
Publisher: ButterflyMan Publishing LLC

Preface — Why Pakistan Needs a Rebirth of the Soul

Pakistan does not merely need a new government.
It needs a new soul.

For more than seventy years, this land has been trapped between division,
war, poverty, and corruption.
Yet the real problem lies not in its economy or its army,
but in the human heart —
where fear replaced faith,
obedience replaced reason,
and hatred replaced compassion.

This book is not a political manifesto.
It is a blueprint for civilizational reconstruction.

It asks a simple question:

> If faith is the light of truth,
> why is our world still covered in darkness?

> Because when faith loses justice, it becomes the servant of power;
> and when justice loses faith, it becomes a cold instrument of law.

Future of Pakistan is a journey of the soul —
from fear to belief,
from domination to covenant,
from punishment to compassion.

Table of Contents

Structure of the Book

Chapter 1 – First Impressions: Between Faith and Poverty

The author's first encounters in Pakistan —
the smiles on the streets, the hope in young faces,
and a nation suspended between corruption and kindness.
The contrast between the people's warmth and the system's cruelty
sets the stage for the entire book.

Chapter 2 – The Roots of Corruption: When Power Replaces Faith

An analysis of structural corruption and the politicization of religion.
How obedience has replaced moral responsibility,
and how fear has been weaponized as a tool of "stability."

Chapter 3 – The Silence of the People: From Fear to Numbness

Decades of repression have bred resignation.
Through interviews with workers, students, and women,
this chapter captures the psychology of a nation forced into quiet
endurance.

Chapter 4 – Awakening of Youth: A New Dialogue Between Education and Faith

How young Pakistanis use technology, art, and creativity
to challenge conformity and reclaim meaning.
A poetic portrait of a generation refusing to memorize other people's
answers.

Chapter 5 – Faith and Power: The Divine Test

A critique of how religion has been misused to legitimize political control.
A call to return to the true spirit of Islam —
justice, compassion, freedom, and truth.

Chapter 6 – The Birth of Democracy: From Obedience to Participation

Democracy is not an event, but a way of life.
When people learn to question, reason, and act,
reform becomes irreversible.
Introduces the concept of the "Day of Return to the People"
and the Citizen's Handbook for Renewal.

Chapter 7 – Preparing for True Transformation

Defines the three foundations of sustainable change:
Truth, Trust, and Institutions.
Proposes synchronized reform in education, media, justice, and religious
interpretation —
and sketches the inner vision of a free, peaceful, and equal Pakistan.

Chapter 8 – Rebuilding Institutions: Making the People the Foundation of the State

From centralization to local autonomy.
From the pyramid of power to the network of citizens.
Outlines a new constitutional vision:
independent judiciary, free press, universal healthcare, and education for all.

Chapter 9 – The Social Covenant: From Trust to Institution

Explores how a citizen society is born.

Its three pillars: Transparency, Accountability, and Participation.
Shows how youth, women, media, and faith can share responsibility
in sustaining democracy.

"Democracy is not the day you vote — it is every day after."

Chapter 10 – Rebirth of Civilization: Faith and Humanity in Harmony

The philosophical summit of the book.
Describes the final evolution from fear-based rule to compassion-based
civilization.
When faith and reason embrace,
God's kingdom begins — not in heaven, but in the human heart.

Core Principles

Domain	Central Idea	Interpretation
Faith	Faith is conscience, not submission	"God commands justice, kindness, and the keeping of covenants."
Governance	Power must serve the people	Constitution above men; accountability above obedience
Education	Teach thinking, not memorizing	Critical reasoning as spiritual practice
Economy	Equity and integrity	Dignity of labor + ethics of enterprise
Society	Empathy bound to law	Equality, women's rights, inter-sect respect
Future	Civilization built on compassion	Integration of technology, morality, and justice

The Mirage of Iron Brotherhood: Authoritarian Alliances and the Absence of Public Legitimacy in Modernization

Chapter M1 – Introduction: The Myth of the Iron Brotherhood

The phrase "iron brotherhood" is exposed as a political illusion — a myth of
unity masking control.

Through his arrival scene and forced escort, the author reveals how friendship becomes surveillance,
and how "solidarity" between authoritarian states often means dependency dressed as diplomacy.
This chapter establishes the book's central question:
can a relationship built on fear ever call itself brotherhood?

Chapter M2 – Five Days in Lahore: The Boundaries of Friendship

The author's fieldwork in Lahore reveals a society of warmth constrained by invisible walls.
Factories hum with diligence, yet Chinese workers remain hidden and guarded.
The refrain "it's the rule" encapsulates the quiet tyranny of habit over law.
Economic hardship and social fatigue overshadow talk of politics —
showing how fear drains not just courage, but imagination.

Chapter M3 – Fear in the Night: The Passport Incident

A late-night confrontation at a checkpoint turns into a portrait of systemic fear.
When soldiers confiscate the author's passport, dignity itself is suspended.
The small detour on Lahore's empty road becomes a metaphor for a nation's detour from freedom.
If this is how guests are treated, what of its citizens?
The logic of control replaces the logic of respect.

Chapter M4 – From Personal Experience to Institutional Reflection

The narrative widens from the personal to the structural.
Two Pakistans emerge — one humane, one militarized.
The officer's act of seizing the passport is reframed as a symptom of a power-conditioned reflex.
The military's reach into economy, media, and law transforms society into a garrison.

Development, under such command, becomes an instrument of discipline, not progress.

Chapter M5 – China's Mirror: The Illusion of Brotherhood

The author turns the lens inward, confronting China's complicity.
Projects under the banner of "brotherhood" are revealed as fortresses of control —
militarized zones that exclude the very people they claim to uplift.
He argues that Beijing's exported authoritarianism mirrors its domestic insecurities.
Buying silence through infrastructure is not stability — it is fear wearing a mask of development.

Chapter M6 – A Warning to Pakistan's Military

A direct address to the generals:
Fear is not order, and weapons are not dignity.
The army's dominance has smothered Pakistan's civic heart.
When soldiers define law, the nation loses its conscience.
The author warns that no regime can imprison history,
and urges the military to step back before fear corrodes the state beyond repair.

Chapter M7 – Return to Humanity and Rights

Here the book reclaims the moral ground.
True modernity lies not in megaprojects but in the restoration of human rights and public trust.
A friendship that requires guns is no friendship at all.
The chapter envisions a new civic foundation —
where law restrains power, and sovereignty belongs to the people.
The author's call: lay down fear, and rise as citizens.

Conclusion – The Collapse of a Fear-Based Alliance

The passport incident becomes the symbol of a broader collapse.
The "iron brotherhood" crumbles under its contradictions —
alliances built on repression cannot survive freedom.
As the plane lifts into the night, the author reflects:
"Fear ends where faith begins."
The ultimate faith lies not in armies or governments,
but in the enduring will of people to reclaim their dignity.

Structure of the Special Issue

Chapter S1 — Introduction: The Myth of the Iron Brotherhood

Core idea: The slogan of "iron-like friendship" masks a model of cooperation built on regime-to-regime trust, military protection, and social exclusion— producing modernization without legitimacy.
Key points:
- Rhetoric vs. reality: "shared destiny" vs. sealed zones and escorted movement
- Friendship as vigilance: security theaters at airports, compounds, and project sites
- People as spectators: citizens excluded from decisions and benefits
- Modernization dilemma: visible infrastructure, invisible trust
- Thesis: authoritarian cooperation substitutes control for integration, fear for legitimacy

Chapter S2 — Literature Review & Theoretical Framework

Core idea: A synthesis of authoritarian mutual assistance, developmentalism traps, securitization, elite capture, and discursive power to analyze "securitized friendship."

Key points:

- Authoritarian mutualism: regimes outsource legitimacy (Levitsky & Way; Slater; Diamond)
- Developmentalism trap: "embedded autonomy" collapses into isolated bureaucracy (Johnson; Evans; Basu; Rolland)
- Securitization: cooperation militarized; debate foreclosed (Buzan/Wæver/de Wilde; Siddiqa)
- Elite capture: opaque contracts, upward absorption of rents (Klitgaard; TI data)
- Discourse & ritual: "brotherhood" as emotional governance (Foucault; Hull)
- Analytical lens: Power Mutualism / Development Illusion / Discursive Control → Institutional Mirage

Chapter S3 — Power Mechanisms & the Operational Logic of Securitized Friendship

Core idea: Military–bureaucratic dominance converts external cooperation into an internal control project.

Key points:

- Parallel state: military as economic gatekeeper and policy arbiter (Siddiqa)
- File politics: approvals and secrecy as performances of authority (Hull; Levitsky & Way)
- Security enclaves: fortified development that segregates people and capital (Rolland)
- Closed loop: loans → subcontracting to aligned elites → socialized debt
- Opinion architecture: performative friendship, silenced public (Diamond)
- Fear cycle: Fear → Protection → Dependency → brittle stability (Slater)

Chapter S4 — The Economic Mirage & Social Dependency

Core idea: High-visibility projects create statistical prosperity but stagnating livelihoods and mounting debt.

Key points:

- Engineering legitimacy: GDP spectacle over welfare outcomes (Basu)
- Debt politics: constrained sovereignty via opaque loans (Rolland; Klitgaard; TI)
- Jobs paradox: large GDP share, minimal employment absorption (ILO patterns)
- Elite redistribution: oligarchic capture of rents; squeezed middle class
- Erosion of hope: trust curdles into indifference; legitimacy hollows out (Evans)
- Institutional aphasia: "development" replaces "rights/justice/citizenship"

Chapter S5 — Cultural & Discursive Mirage: Language, Propaganda, and the Breakdown of Trust

Core idea: The language of "brotherhood" manufactures emotional consent while deepening social distance.

Key points:

- Words as power: slogans create moralized obedience (Foucault)
- Emotional governance: unity via external threat narratives (Diamond; Slater)
- Spatial othering: two worlds—secure corridors vs. local streets (Hull)
- Identity politicized: passport/appearance as security signals
- Religious veneer: faith instrumentalized for legitimacy, compassion hollowed
- Visual politics: curated images normalize a fictive stability (Rolland) → trust collapses

Chapter S6 — From Fear to Hope: A Night When Military Power Replaced Law

Core idea: The Aziz Bhatti Road passport seizure is a microcosm of rule-by-fear—and the spark for civic awakening.

Key points:
- Event anatomy: unlawful confiscation, forced detour, no accountability
- Systemic reading: colonial reflexes → military primacy; legality subordinated
- Social psychology: fear as common language; obedience rebranded as patriotism
- Civic line in the sand: consular reporting and formal protest as defense of norms
- Development cost: militarization depresses growth and trust
- Arc of renewal: dignified anger → rational action → nonviolent civic rebuilding

Chapter S7 — Rebuilding Institutions: Truth, Trust, and Law as Roots of the Nation

Core idea: Move from securitized fraternity to institutional friendship through truth-telling, participation, and rule of law.

Key points:
- Truth infrastructure: investigations, whistleblower protection, open data (Klitgaard)
- Trust architecture: equality before law, civic participation, critical education
- Rule-of-law baselines: judicial independence, civilian oversight, constitutional literacy
- Decentralization: fiscal/local autonomy; community-led social programs
- Moral modernization: conscience over propaganda; fairness over privilege (Basu)

- International turn: replace "iron brotherhood" with institutional friendship (law, exchange, trust)
- Coda: "Fear ends where faith begins—fulfilled only when law protects the weak."

From Suharto to Reformasi—and Beyond: Lessons for Pakistan from Indonesia's Democratic Transition

Indonesia and Pakistan, both populous Muslim-majority nations with post-colonial histories and long experiences of military or authoritarian dominance, diverged sharply after 1998. Indonesia's transition from the Suharto "New Order" to the Reformasi era of decentralised democracy has produced tangible economic and social gains. Pakistan, meanwhile, remains constrained by recurrent military interventions and fragile civilian institutions. This article presents a comparative analysis of their political economies, cultural structures, and governance systems. It argues that Indonesia's model—crisis-triggered reform, institutional decentralisation, and gradual civil–military rebalancing—offers critical lessons for Pakistan's democratic and developmental future.

THE RIGHT TO REFUSE

Military obedience has long been regarded as the cornerstone of discipline and state security. Yet history demonstrates that blind obedience, untempered by conscience or law, can transform an army from a national protector into an instrument of internal oppression. From Latin America's military juntas to the Middle East's praetorian regimes, and from Southeast Asia to Africa, soldiers have repeatedly been ordered to suppress their own people in the name of stability. This article advances a new global doctrine: the Right and Duty of Lawful Refusal, whereby soldiers are constitutionally empowered to reject, resist, or act in self-defense against manifestly unlawful domestic orders. Drawing upon comparative case studies from Indonesia, Pakistan, Myanmar, Cambodia, Egypt, Nigeria, Chile, and Brazil, the paper situates this principle within democratic theory, international humanitarian law, and military professionalism. It proposes a model constitutional clause — integrating lawful refusal, self-defense, and commander accountability — as a universal safeguard against authoritarian relapse. The argument reframes military professionalism as fidelity to constitutional law rather than to rulers, thereby uniting discipline with moral courage. The study concludes that institutionalizing this principle is essential for any modern democracy seeking to reconcile security with human dignity.

Keywords: Civil–Military Relations, Constitutional Reform, Lawful Refusal, Military Ethics, Democratic Transition, Global South

Chapter 1 — The Beginning of Awakening
— *The Warmth of an Unknown Land*

1. First Encounter: Between Faith and the System

This was my first time in Pakistan.
No matter how many problems the country still faces, its system of
universal healthcare remains an admirable achievement.
Perhaps it arises from the compassion for life found in religion,
or perhaps it was merely a way for a harsh regime to win people's hearts.
Whatever the motive, the system's existence has indeed saved many lives.

What struck me most was the warmth and sincerity of the Pakistani people.
There were traces of poverty and oppression in their smiles,
yet they still carried kindness toward strangers,
an instinct for justice, and a quiet endurance toward fate.
Almost everyone knew of the corruption and cruelty of the military
government,
yet they were not consumed by hatred;
they lived with gentleness and dignity.

Their eyes told me this:
Human nature has not been erased by oppression—only put to sleep for a
time.
And that tenderness is the deepest strength of this country.

2. A Smile in the Café

At noon, I had lunch in a small café.
A young girl walked over to my table,
shyly asking if she could take a photo with me.
For a moment, I hesitated, afraid of being misunderstood,
but soon realized she was simply curious and kind.

I smiled and invited her back to take the picture.

Her friends gathered around, laughing brightly.
At that moment, the tension within me loosened—
I realized that this Muslim country, often misunderstood by outsiders,
was in fact filled with natural openness and human warmth.

In that instant, I thought:
True civilization is not measured by the height of buildings,
but by the freedom that allows strangers to smile at one another.

3. The Driver in the Night

That night, I took a ride with a young driver.
He had studied architecture but, three years after graduating, still couldn't
find stable work.
He had a wife and two children,
and earned less than six hundred dollars a month.

I invited him to dinner.
He declined at first, then sat down shyly.
As we ate, he spoke of inequality, corruption, and the struggle of daily life.
His tone was calm but sincere—
it was the voice of a man who *sees the truth and still chooses to live.*

I asked, "Do you still believe in the future?"
He paused, then smiled faintly:

"We have to believe—otherwise we couldn't go on."

That sentence stayed with me.
Perhaps the hope of a nation lies in such a smile—
not in blind optimism, but in the unextinguished faith that survives
hardship.

4. The Lobby at Midnight

By the time dinner was over, it was deep into the night.

When I returned to the hotel, a dozen fourteen-year-old boys were sitting in the lobby.
They had just finished a science competition and were preparing to buy ice cream.

I smiled and asked, "It's so late—aren't you going to sleep?"
They replied, "We have to celebrate after the competition!"
I said, "Shall I treat you?"
They shook their heads immediately: "You're a guest. That wouldn't be right."

In that moment, I saw a pure sense of dignity.
In a country of material scarcity,
they still understood self-respect and principle—
and that is the real hope of a nation.

5. A Conversation with the Boys

I asked them, "Who wants to be a soldier?"
They replied together, "No one—the army is corrupt."
I asked again, "Then what will you do when you grow up?"
Without hesitation, they said, "Work abroad."

I laughed and asked, "If you all leave, who will change your country?"

Silence fell.
They looked at one another, serious for the first time.

I took out my phone and opened an article I had just finished writing—
a piece later included in *The Future of* Pakistan as similar to future of china series

I read it aloud to them.

Return to Democracy — Hope for a Civic Future

Pakistan's ultimate hope lies in the peaceful redistribution of power.
For decades, the military has called itself the *guardian of national stability.*
But when it finally understands that stability is born not of fear but of legitimacy,
true transformation will begin.

When the army relinquishes control over politics and the economy,
when power is returned to the people through free and fair elections,
the structure of trust will be rebuilt.
Civilian government will regain both moral and functional authority,
and entrepreneurs, educators, and professionals
will be free to create without fear of arbitrary interference.

Such a change will not weaken the nation—
it will save it.
The military will return to its constitutional duty of defense,
and the republic will be able to devote its energy
to education, welfare, and prosperity.

History has already shown:
A nation's greatness lies not in the power of its generals,
but in the people's capacity for self-governance.
Pakistan's true modernization
is not in new dams, missiles, or apps,
but in the simplest yet most revolutionary act—
returning power to the people.

Conclusion: Between System and Soul

The electronic visa that arrived several days late
was more than a travel inconvenience—
it was a mirror,
reflecting how a nation can let "purpose" be replaced by "procedure,"
and "service" by "suspicion."

Yet within this confusion lies immense potential.
There are educated youths, connected to the world yet filled with frustration;
entrepreneurs who keep innovating despite constraints;
citizens who take pride in endurance rather than privilege—
these are the people who embody Pakistan's hope.

As the experience of Bangladesh shows,
reform begins at the moment a government dares to trust its people.
Pakistan's future does not lie in the next *Vision 2025*,
but in a moral modernization—
turning fear into trust,
and control into capability.

When visas, licenses, and permits cease to symbolize suspicion
and instead represent service and trust,
Pakistan's soul will awaken once again.

Epilogue: The Boys and the Future

When I finished reading, I looked at the boys.
They sat quietly, eyes bright with light.

I said to them:

> "Rebuild confidence, reclaim your civic rights.
> Reject fear, refuse meaningless sacrifice.
> This country should be yours.
> Forgive the corrupt, rebuild the system,
> and return society to the hands of the people.
> Pakistan belongs to its young."

They nodded and smiled.
Before leaving, they asked to take a group photo.
In that moment, I was deeply moved.

I believe that one day
Pakistan will return to the embrace of its people.
And the ones who bring that change
will not be generals or bureaucrats,
but these hopeful children—
still untainted by the system.

Chapter 2 — The Structure of Power and Fear
— In the Name of "Stability"

1. The Engineered Fear

In Pakistan, when people speak of politics, the first word is rarely *freedom*
— it is *danger*.
This danger does not come from foreign invasion or war,
but from a deeply rooted *institutional fear*:
fear of power, fear of the government, fear of losing one's job, identity, or
trust.

At the airport visa counter, before the guard at a checkpoint, or when a
military truck passes by on the street,
that fear becomes tangible and physical.
It does not require violence — because the shadow of violence already lives
inside every mind.

> "Don't challenge, and you'll survive. Stay silent, and you'll be safe."
> This is the creed the entire system subtly implants into its citizens.

> Fear is not innate.
> It is a carefully engineered social structure.
> A nation that worships "security above all"
> often robs its people of the most precious human rights —
> the right to question and the right to choose.

2. The Colonial Legacy: The Myth of the Military

The Pakistani military is not merely an armed institution — it is a
psychological symbol.
During the colonial era, the British fused military and administration into a
system of *politics by order*,
turning obedience into the supreme civic virtue.

After independence, that structure did not dissolve; it became even more deeply embedded in the state.

Each time a political crisis arose,
the army intervened under the banner of "saving the nation."
A coup ceased to be seen as a seizure of power;
it was repackaged as a sacred act of "stabilization" and "salvation."
Soldiers were mythologized as "fathers of the nation,"
while the people were treated perpetually as children — to be managed and instructed.

In such a culture, obedience masquerades as order,
and fear disguises itself as safety.
The military's presence seeps into education, media, religion, commerce, even the arts.
An invisible message reverberates through society:

"Without the military, you would be destroyed."

3. The Illusion of the System

In Pakistan, fear does not always appear as repression.
More often, it is wrapped in the language of "care" and "protection."
If you question the efficiency of the government, you are reminded,

"It's for national security."
If you criticize corruption, you are warned,
"Don't let foreign powers use your words."

The rhetoric of the system has become so familiar that people forget:
true security is not surveillance,
but the ability of citizens to trust one another.

Another form of fear lies in *the labyrinth of bureaucracy.*
From e-visas and business licenses to school admissions,
every procedure whispers the same truth:

Power does not belong to you; it belongs to those who approve you.

People learn patience through waiting,
silence through patience,
and self-censorship through silence.
That is the most insidious triumph of power —
it no longer needs violence, because the people have internalized its rules.

4. The Economics of Fear

Fear is not just a psychological condition — it is an *economic structure.*
When poverty and instability become everyday realities,
fear becomes the cheapest and most effective tool of social control.

Young people dream of leaving, not because they hate their land,
but because the system has erased the very idea of change.
Entrepreneurs hesitate to innovate because policies shift overnight;
intellectuals remain silent because truth invites punishment.

Fear breeds dependence, and dependence breeds obedience.
The stability of power is maintained through this *psychological taxation.*
What you pay is not only money — it is hope.

5. The Mirror of Comparison: The Shadow of China

Within this structure, Pakistan and China reveal a startling resemblance.
Both prioritize "collective stability" over "individual freedom."
Both use "patriotism" as the moral cloak for corruption.

China's party-state system manufactures fear through ideology;
Pakistan's military system sustains obedience through the myth of security.
One replaces the nation with the Party,
the other replaces the people with the Army.

Both share the same conviction:

> "People must be ruled,"
> instead of
> "People can rule themselves."

> Yet history proves the opposite —
> the truly strong nations are not those whose citizens fear their governments,
> but those whose governments *fear their citizens.*

6. The Culture of Fear

Fear does not live only in institutions — it seeps into culture and language.
In schools, children are taught to "obey," not to "think."
In families, obedience is praised as virtue, while questioning is condemned as rebellion.
In sermons, divine authority is often extended to justify political power.

Thus, society evolves a *vertical way of thinking*:
everyone looks upward for permission
instead of sideways for consensus.
In such a culture,
freedom itself becomes a nameless form of fear.

And yet, that is precisely why courage becomes so valuable.
A single young person who dares to say "no"
may stand closer to the nation's hope
than a general who commands an army.

7. The First Step to Breaking Fear

To break fear is not to start a revolution — it is to begin *education.*
When people truly understand the meaning of the phrase

> "Power is granted by the people,"

the architecture of fear begins to crumble.

The starting point of reform lies not in the barracks, nor in parliament,
but in the heart of every citizen who refuses silence.
Fear is powerful only because people believe it cannot be changed;
the moment someone dares to stop believing, it begins to collapse.

Pakistan's future does not depend on whether the generals yield power,
but on whether its youth choose to stay.
When *leaving* is no longer the only option,
staying becomes an act of courage.

8. Epilogue: From Fear to Trust

Fear is an invisible prison.
Its walls are not made of steel, but of the mind.

The only path forward for this nation is the rebuilding of *trust.*
Let the army return to defense,
let the government return to service,
let education return to enlightenment rather than domestication.
This is not merely the reconstruction of institutions —
it is the rebirth of a nation's soul.

One day, when the people no longer fear their government,
and when the young dare to stay and create the future,
then Pakistan will truly be free.

Because genuine stability
is never built upon fear —
it is built upon trust and dignity.

Chapter 3 — The Architecture of Poverty: Trapped Between Hope and Despair

— *When a Society Forgets How to Dream*

1) Poverty Is Not Just a Lack of Money

On Pakistan's streets, poverty is an air you can touch.
At intersections in Karachi and Lahore, you'll often see dust-covered children—
a water bottle in one hand, the other tapping on car windows, asking for a few coins.
There is habit in their smiles, and there is fatigue.

Scenes like this are not unusual.
What is unusual is that such reality is treated as "normal."
From the car window, the urban middle class passes out a note—
satisfying compassion while preserving the order of things.

Poverty long ago ceased to be only material deprivation;
it is a designed fate, institutionalized.
The poor are assigned to uphold the moral balance of the entire system:
their existence lets the rich feel benevolent;
allows the government to claim it is "still fighting poverty";
and gives religious institutions a stage for "holy charity."

It is a grand illusion—
in which everyone believes themselves good,
and no one asks:
Why do the poor never disappear?

2) Middle-Class Anxiety: The Polite Prison

I met a young engineer
living in a bare rental on the outskirts of Lahore.
Each morning he rode a battered motorbike to work;

his wages barely kept his wife and child afloat.

"We're not poor," he said, "but we can't afford to get sick."
That sentence was a needle piercing the polished veneer of respectability.

In Pakistan, the middle class is not a stabilizing force;
it is the buffer wedged between fear and poverty.
Educated—yet powerless to change reality.
Aware of corruption—yet afraid to speak.
Terrified of falling into poverty, and unable to become truly free.

Their deepest anxiety is not low income;
it is the awareness that "no matter how hard we try, nothing changes."
This is poverty of the mind:
knowing injustice, but being forced to accept it;
knowing change is needed, but choosing silence.

3) The Illusion of Education

In poor countries, education is painted as the lone road out of fate.
But in Pakistan, education itself has become a ritual of class reproduction.

The wealthy send children to English-medium schools and international curricula;
the poor memorize Qur'an verses and history in overcrowded public schools.
Teachers are underpaid, textbooks outdated, classrooms dim.
Children learn not to think, but to obey.

A young factory worker told me:
"My parents sold our land so I could study.
Now I'm more educated than they are—yet I earn less."

Education becomes a vast illusion.
It teaches people that hope exists,
while reality keeps proving that—
knowledge, too, is monopolized by power.

Under such a system, education is no tool of liberation;
it is a shackle that cements class.

4) Faith's Double Role

From every corner of every city, the call to prayer rises.
It soothes—and it lulls.

Faith grants dignity to the poor,
and legitimacy to those who rule.
"This is God's decree" becomes the most common explanation for injustice.
Donation boxes, fasting, almsgiving...
Religion sustains a moral sense—
even as it dampens the impulse to reform.

An imam in a mosque told me,
"Endure, and heaven will bring justice."
I smiled, but thought:
If heaven delays,
shouldn't people create justice themselves?

Faith should awaken the heart;
used by power, it extends fear.
Compassion without action becomes anesthesia.

5) The Aid Trap

Whenever international news mentions Pakistan,
it is almost always accompanied by "IMF loans" or "foreign aid."
Aid is packaged as salvation—
but in practice it prolongs poverty.

To qualify for loans, the state cuts public spending, freezes wages;
education and health budgets shrink;
and the poor pay for the debt—again.

Foreign institutions, NGOs, and governments,
together with local political and business elites, form an "aid economy."
Money circulates, reports are written, results are showcased—
and poverty on the streets stands still.

Aid becomes a new colonial form:
money instead of armies, conditions instead of occupation.
It doesn't change reality; it keeps order intact.

6) Women: The Silent Pillar

In every Pakistani household,
women are the quiet, indispensable support.

Up at dawn to cook, care for children, wash clothes;
some sew in factories by day, others embroider from home.
Their labor sustains the daily life of the social base—
yet they are rarely counted as "workers."

In some urban neighborhoods, I saw girls slipping into night classes,
hoping someday to become nurses or teachers.
There was no romantic dreaming in their eyes—
only a steady resolve: "My fate will not be decided by others."

When a society ignores women,
it forfeits half its future.

Real progress is not men earning more money;
it is women free to choose their lives.

7) Two Roads for the Young

Late at night, cafés fill with students and young professionals.
They talk startups, tech, AI, design—
and how to secure a visa out.

"Leaving" becomes a synonym for freedom.
Those who stay are often those who cannot leave.

This is Pakistan's deepest tragedy:
it is not only knowledge that leaves—
hope leaves with it.

But there is another group.
They choose to stay.
They build social enterprises, open schools, teach children to code,
extend microloans so women can start businesses.
"If we all go," they say,
"who will change this place?"

They are the quiet rebels of a fear-based system.
No slogans. Just action.

8) A Dignity Economy: Making a Living by One's Work

An old farmer told me,
"We don't need charity—we just need to sell what we make."
That sentence outweighs a thousand policy papers.

Real economic reform
is not more aid or grand new plans;
it is making it possible to live by one's labor.

The core of a dignity economy is this:
not alms, but fairness;
not dependency, but creation.

Give farmers secure rights to land;
workers union power and social protection;
youth a chance to found businesses without being plundered;
women education and the freedom to work.

Only then can a nation become truly wealthy—

not only in money, but in dignity.

9) Conclusion: From the Edge of Despair, a Glance Back at Hope

The cruellest thing about poverty
is not material lack—
it is the way it teaches helplessness.

The real revolution is not the sound of guns;
it is the moment a poor person realizes—
poverty is not their fault.

That is the beginning of awakening.
When people start to believe, "I have a right to a better life,"
a nation's fate begins to turn.

Pakistan's future is not in foreign aid or the calculus of generals;
it is in every person who refuses numbness and still dares to dream.

Their dreams are the country's new currency.
When dreaming is permitted again,
hope will circulate once more.

Chapter 4 — The Cage of Education and the Liberation of Thought
— *When Knowledge Becomes a Tool of Domestication*

1. From "School" to "System"

In Pakistan, on a child's first day of school,
they are not taught how to think — but how to obey.
They are instructed on how to recite, how to pray, how not to make mistakes.
Error is not the beginning of learning; it is treated as shame.

On classroom walls hang the Prophet's sayings, military slogans, and government posters.
Each morning, children sing the national anthem, stand in perfect rows,
and chant the three sacred words: *Loyalty, Faith, Discipline.*

Education — meant to nurture free souls —
has become an extension of power.
Schools are no longer places that cultivate thought;
they have become factories that reproduce obedience.

2. The Ghost of Colonialism

Pakistan's education system was born under the shadow of empire.
The British left behind an examination regime, a class-based school hierarchy, and a diploma structure —
essentially, a mechanism for social selection.

It allowed a small minority to rise into positions of authority
through "the right language" and "the right credentials,"
while excluding everyone else.

After independence, this structure was not dismantled —
it was perfected.
The military government and elite class learned to use it skillfully.

English-medium education became the badge of class;
to *speak English* meant refinement,
to speak only Urdu meant inferiority.

Language turned into a new chain of class,
and knowledge became the passport to power.

3. Religion and the State: A Pact of Control

In Pakistan, religion and education are inseparable.
Madrasas — mosque-based schools — provide the most basic form of learning,
but also serve as fertile ground for state control over thought.

Children are taught to memorize scripture, not to understand it;
to submit to divine will, not to question human authority.
Such education breeds citizens who are *pious but passive.*

The state skillfully exploits religious authority,
binding political loyalty and faith loyalty together.
Thus, "not questioning the government"
and "not questioning God"
become subconsciously one and the same.

When the sacred and the political unite,
the air for free thought disappears.

4. Lies in the Textbooks

I once examined Pakistan's secondary school history textbooks.
There were no chapters of reflection —
only "glorious wars," "national purity," and "victories of faith."

India is the enemy, the West a threat;
the nation, forever a victim forced to defend itself.
And the soldier — eternally the hero.

The danger of this narrative is not that it is false,
but that it leaves no room to imagine any other truth.

When a child is taught from an early age that *to question is to betray*,
the adult society that follows can only consist of obedience and silence.

The language of textbooks is the most invisible prison of power.
It needs no police, no censorship.
For once a mind has been schooled,
it learns to lock its own doors.

5. The Teacher's Dilemma

A high school teacher in Lahore told me,

> "It's not that we don't want to teach critical thinking — it's that no one
> wants to hear it."

> Teachers are underpaid, classrooms overcrowded, materials outdated.
> Worse still — they are monitored.
> If a lesson touches on politics, gender, or religious freedom,
> a parent or official might report them at any moment.

> So teachers learn self-censorship.
> They teach only the truths that are safe,
> and keep the meaningful questions to themselves.

> Education thus falls into a vicious cycle:
> students dare not ask, teachers dare not answer,
> and knowledge becomes *safe memorization*.

6. The Illusion of the Degree

In Pakistan, the degree has become a social status symbol.
Every year, tens of thousands graduate from universities —
but fewer than a third find decent employment.

Education is marketed as a path to upward mobility,
but in truth, it is another trap of competition.
The rich study abroad and inherit companies;
ordinary youth carry student debt
and wait in coffee shops for calls that never come.

Knowledge has been commodified;
the diploma is a consumer identity.
And thought — grows ever cheaper.

7. The Sealing of Thought

"Free thought" is a dangerous phrase in this society.
Too many intellectuals have been silenced, disappeared, or exiled
for criticizing the military or religion.

Fear has made academia timid.
Professors avoid political topics with surgical precision;
students learn to trade silence for safety.

Universities, which should be sanctuaries of liberated thought,
have become warehouses of *safe knowledge.*
People learn how to calculate, but forget how to reason;
they learn how to speak, but not how to tell the truth.

When knowledge loses courage,
it ceases to be knowledge — it becomes mere information.

8. The Beginning of Liberation: Learning to Ask "Why"

True educational reform is not about building more schools;
it is about teaching children to ask questions again.

A society that cannot tolerate *why*
will never move forward.

Why can't we criticize the government?
Why can't girls receive equal education?
Why does poverty repeat itself?
Why must truth have only one voice?

These questions are not merely the start of education —
they are the start of freedom.

To liberate thought is not to deny faith;
it is to let faith and reason coexist.
It is not to destroy tradition;
it is to allow tradition to face honest examination.

9. The Sparks of a New Generation

In my conversations with Pakistan's youth,
I am often moved by the quiet defiance in their spirit.
Though their reality is harsh, they still hunger to learn, think, and create.

Some teach themselves programming online;
some form small reading circles
and discuss science and society in rooms behind mosques;
others make short films with cheap phones,
trying to show the world another Pakistan.

They no longer wait for "reform" to descend from above —
they are rebuilding spaces of thought from below.
These young people
are igniting faint yet genuine sparks
in a society suffocated by fear and silence.

They remind me that free thought
is never born of institutions —
it begins the moment someone dares to say,

"I disagree."

10. Conclusion: The Redemption of Education

The true purpose of education
is not to make people successful,
but to make them awake.

When schools teach obedience above all,
then true education must begin *outside* the school.

Perhaps Pakistan's hope
will not come from government policy,
but from the children studying alone at night,
the teachers who persist in broken classrooms,
and the young people thinking aloud online.

They are using thought
to open a new window for the nation.

Because only the liberation of thought
can bring freedom to the soul.

Chapter 5 — The Boundary Between Faith and Humanity: When Religion Meets Democracy

— *Beyond the Sacred, the Human Heart Must Remain*

1. The Light of Faith

In Pakistan, faith is the rhythm of daily life.
At dawn, the call to prayer awakens entire cities.
The rich and the poor alike turn toward the same direction in worship.

In that chorus of unity, people become briefly equal.
Here, faith is not merely religion—
it is a shared breath, a thread that binds the social fabric.

I have walked through markets, factories, and campuses,
and seen how, even amid hardship, people retain kindness.
They may earn little, yet share their food;
they may live under oppression, yet still give thanks to God.

This is the gentle strength of Islamic civilization:
amid extreme poverty and injustice,
faith allows humanity to survive.

2. The Corruption of the Sacred

But when religion is seized by power,
the sacred begins to decay.

In Pakistan, politics and religion are nearly inseparable.
Generals quote the Qur'an in speeches;
politicians call themselves "guardians of faith";
clerics sit as advisers in parliament,
draping political decisions in divine legitimacy.

Faith should humble the human spirit,

but reflected in the mirror of power,
it becomes a tool of justification.
"To oppose the government is to oppose God"—
once such an idea is accepted,
all dissent becomes blasphemy.

Faith ceases to be a personal choice
and turns into a political duty.

3. The Theology of Fear

Power loves religion because it can turn obedience into virtue.

In many schools, children are taught from early on:
"God knows all, God judges all."
This could be a moral reminder,
but when used to uphold authority,
it becomes an invisible chain.

People act righteously not out of belief,
but out of fear of punishment.
They obey not from love,
but from the instinct to survive.

This fear-based piety
fills society with devotion—
but empties it of spiritual freedom.

4. The Misalignment of God and the State

Pakistan's constitution is founded upon Islam,
but there is a vast difference between
a *religious state* and a *faithful society.*

A religious state rules people in the name of God;
a faithful society honors God through the dignity of humanity.

The former places divine law above human rights;
the latter builds morality upon the foundation of faith.

The issue is not Islam itself,
but the courage to ask—
where should the line between the sacred and the political lie?

When politics loses balance, the sacred becomes corrupted.
When faith becomes a servant of power,
people lose the freedom to speak with God.

5. Two Faces of Faith

Throughout my travels, I met two kinds of Muslims.

One kind is devout and open-minded—
after prayer, they discuss democracy, science, and human rights.
They believe that faith should guide, not imprison.

The other kind is equally devout,
but treats religion as a fortress.
They fear difference,
fear women's freedom, fear intellectual debate,
and even fear sharing a meal with foreigners
lest they be thought impure.

These two faces reflect the tug-of-war within Pakistan's soul:
on one side, compassionate Islam;
on the other, politicized Islam.
True faith, perhaps, now lies trapped between the two.

6. Women's Faith: Patience and Awakening

In many mosques, women's prayer spaces are walled off.
In many villages, girls' education is considered unnecessary.

Yet I have seen another reality:
young mothers teaching their children both Qur'an and English at home.
They tell me,

"God gave us minds not only to obey, but to understand."

Such words are soft, yet profoundly strong.
They do not confront religion from the outside,
but illuminate its darkness from within.

The awakening of women
is the most subtle—and most genuine—force
for religious reform in Pakistan.

7. The Future of Religion: From Monopoly to Coexistence

True faith does not fear diversity.
Diversity is not disrespect to God;
it is reverence for the vastness of His creation.

When a society allows different sects to coexist,
when minority religions can pray without fear,
that is the mark of mature faith.

Religion and democracy are not natural enemies.
Religion provides the moral foundation;
democracy ensures that no one may monopolize God's voice.

Together, they can give birth to a society
both ethical and free.

8. From Fear to Understanding

The highest form of faith is not blind reverence,
but conscious understanding.

Reverence makes us humble;
understanding makes us free.

For Pakistan to become truly modern,
it must not abandon faith—
but return it to its original essence:
to make people kinder, more responsible,
not more submissive or more easily controlled.

9. The Turning of the Soul

Faith should be a path toward goodness,
not a substitute for reason.

A society where one may believe freely—
and also freely not believe—
is where faith truly triumphs.

Free faith does not weaken religion;
it brings it back to the tenderness at the heart of humanity—
the will to understand others, and to forgive the world.

Epilogue: The Sacred Nation and the Human Future

Pakistan's future lies not in constructing a stricter religious state,
but in restoring religion to the human heart.

True faith is not law, but conscience;
not fear, but understanding;
not punishment, but compassion.

When people stop judging others in God's name
and start understanding the world through human empathy,
then Pakistan will enter its true spiritual freedom.

The Awakening of Power and the Trial of God

**"He made you vicegerents (Khalifah) upon the earth,
that He might test which of you would do good."**
— *Qur'an 6:165*

Power is not a blessing; it is a trial.
Its purpose is not to intoxicate rulers with control,
but to test whether a soul can transcend itself—
to govern with justice and mercy.

When a ruler relies on fear,
his rule is but a fleeting indulgence;
but when he rules with compassion and shares with the people,
his power becomes light, not shadow.

"Do justice; that is closest to piety."
— *Qur'an 5:8*

True piety is not fear of losing power,
but fear of becoming unjust.
A leader who remains humble amid authority,
and remembers equality at the summit of power,
has achieved the true awakening of the soul.

To rejoice with the people is not strategy—
it is faith fulfilled.
To serve the people is not to win votes—
it is to answer God's trust in humankind.

For the highest form of power is not domination—
it is service.

In that moment,
the ruler no longer lives for his own fear,
but acts for the dignity of all.
That is the beginning of true freedom, joy, and salvation—
the root of all blessings in this life and the next.

"Indeed, God does not change the condition of a people until they change what is in their hearts."
— *Qur'an 13:11*

This is where faith and democracy meet:
when humanity learns to restrain power through faith,
and to protect faith through power.
Then, the dawn of Pakistan will no longer arrive
with trumpets or slogans—
but with an inner awakening.

Chapter 6 — The Birth of Democracy: From Obedience to Participation

— *For All Who Still Live in Fear, a Shared Future*

Prologue: A New Vision

When fear withdraws,
freedom ceases to be a dream.
When leaders learn to bow before their people,
history will no longer be written in blood.
When power returns to the hands of the people,
the laughter of children will become the truest anthem of this land.

We must build a new nation—
a community where fear disappears
and faith is never abandoned.
Here, every person—regardless of birth, language, or belief—
shall enjoy equality and liberty;
every person's dignity shall be protected
by both law and society.

To all rulers, exploiters, and the corrupt:
only by voluntarily renouncing privilege
and returning power to the people
can you earn true respect and lasting safety.
Only then can your descendants dwell in peace upon this land,
and only then can you find blessing in the world to come.

This is not a cry of anger—
it is a call of faith.

The Divine Trust

God says in the Qur'an:

"He made you vicegerents (Khalifah) upon the earth,
that He might test which of you would do good."
— *Qur'an 6:165*

This means: Power is not an honor, but a trust.
Those who hold it must walk with mercy as their light
and justice as their path.

If one rules by fear,
the regime will lose God's protection.
But if one governs with compassion,
the people's hearts become the strongest fortress.

God also says:

"Do justice; that is closest to piety."
— *Qur'an 5:8*

Therefore, when those in power
can take justice as their mirror
and humility as their crown,
ceasing to live for their own fear
and instead acting for the dignity of all—
that is the moment of true awakening,
and the peace that God permits.

The Spiritual Birth of Democracy

The birth of democracy is not merely
the replacement of institutions;
it is the transformation of the soul.
It demands awakening in everyone:
that leaders bow to the people,
and the people raise their heads toward conscience.

To rejoice with the people,
to stand equal with the people—

this is not only a political ideal,
but the beginning of personal happiness
and the salvation of the soul.

> **"Indeed, God does not change the condition of a people**
> **until they change what is in their hearts."**
> *— Qur'an 13:11*

When that change comes,
the light of democracy will no longer be a foreign flame—
but the natural sunrise of a nation
that has finally learned to replace fear with faith,
and obedience with participation.

1. From Subjects to Citizens

In Pakistan, history has long been built upon obedience.
From the bureaucratic rule of the colonial era,
to the narrative of "stability" under military regimes,
to the power exchange between religion and political parties—
submission has been regarded as a virtue of survival,
while *resistance* has been labeled as chaos and betrayal.

Such historical conditioning has shaped the psychology of "subjects."
Subjects fear authority and rely on dependence.
They believe more in *fate* than in *rights*,
and more in *obedience* than in *freedom*.

Yet that sense of safety is an illusion.
When people no longer question power,
power learns to plunder.
When a society loses its ability to converse,
its "stability" becomes a silent grave.

The birth of citizenship is never a sudden event,
but a gradual awakening—
when the first person dares to say, *"This is wrong,"*

50

and the second refuses to turn away,
the flame of democracy is lit.

2. The Culture of Fear

"Fear" is a deeply rooted culture.
It lives in families, schools, and workplaces,
and it seeps into the language of politics and religion.

A child is told, *"Don't cause trouble."*
An employee is warned, *"Don't speak your mind."*
A scholar is advised, *"Stay away from politics."*
These small fears intertwine
to form the psychological prison of an entire nation.

Those in power maintain control through fear.
They know: as long as people are afraid,
they will never demand change.

But history never sleeps.
Fear can silence one generation,
but never all generations.
When young people begin to ask *"why,"*
when women demand the right to education,
when workers insist on fair wages—
the wall of fear begins to crack.

3. The Illusion of Power

In Pakistan, power often disguises itself as **"protection."**
The military claims to safeguard stability,
religious leaders claim to defend faith,
and politicians claim to represent the people.

But in truth, these power structures are intertwined—
a vast web sustained by fear.

The rulers convince themselves that
"without us, the country would collapse,"
yet they never ask the real question:
If the people cannot trust their government,
what kind of nation is it?

Power that is not rooted in the people
eventually consumes itself.

True stability does not come from suppression,
but from trust.
And the foundation of trust
is equality and transparency.

4. Misunderstanding Democracy

For many Pakistanis,
"democracy" has been reduced to an election.
People cast their votes—
and then return to passive silence.

But democracy is not a voting system;
it is a way of life.

It is a habit—
a habit of questioning, debating, and participating.
It is a courage—
to speak, even from a place of weakness.
It is a responsibility—
to never hand over one's destiny
to any single person or party.

Democracy is not a perfect system;
it is noisy, messy, and full of contradictions.
But it is precisely this *right to argue*
that keeps a society alive.

5. The Harmony of Faith and Freedom

In a deeply religious nation,
many fear that democracy will weaken faith.
Yet true faith does not fear freedom.

God says in the Qur'an:

> **"If your Lord had willed,**
> **all the people on earth would have believed.**
> **Will you then compel people to believe?"**
> — *Qur'an 10:99*

This verse reveals the essence of freedom:
faith must come from choice, not coercion.
If even God respects human free will,
how can humans, in His name,
deny others their right to choose?

Democracy does not oppose faith.
It simply demands that every person
retain the right to speak with God directly,
and not be forced to let others speak for them.

6. Women, Citizenship, and the Future

A woman in Lahore once told me,
"We are not fighting against men—
we just want to be seen."

She had opened a small sewing studio in her home,
teaching poor girls to make clothes.
She said, "This is my own small democracy."

Her words stayed with me.
The birth of democracy does not begin in parliaments;
it begins in the courage of ordinary women like her.

When more people begin to practice
equality and dignity in their daily lives,
the structure of society itself begins to change.

7. The Power of the Local

Democracy does not grow in capitals;
it grows from villages, communities, mosques, and schools—
from the small habits of shared life.

Real reform does not come
from leaders' generosity,
but from local awakening.

When communities can decide
their own education, healthcare, and budgets,
when local councils can hold the center accountable,
a nation moves from a system of *command*
to a system of *participation.*

This is the transformation Pakistan most urgently needs:
from centralization to local autonomy,
from the ruler's state to the people's nation.

8. The Dual Awakening of Morality and Institutions

The roots of democracy
lie not in the constitution,
but in the moral maturity of the people.

Democracy without morality
is a machine that only counts votes;
morality without institutions
is merely a beautiful wish.

For Pakistan to be reborn,
two structures must be rebuilt—
the outer order of institutions
and the inner order of conscience.

When people respect the law,
and the government obeys it too;
when faith is no longer an excuse for oppression,
but a reminder of compassion—
then democracy will truly take root.

9. The Sovereignty of the People

"The sovereignty of the people" is not a slogan.
It means that every farmer, worker, teacher, student,
mother, and child
is the true owner of the nation.

They have the right to be respected,
the right to be heard,
and the right to change their future.

For those in power,
this truth is not a threat—it is salvation.

Only when they lay down fear,
bow before the people,
and share joy and equality with them,
will they find true safety, respect,
and peace of the soul.

God says:

> **"He does not love the unjust."**
> — *Qur'an 3:57*

> **Its political meaning is profound:**

**true injustice is not losing an election—
it is losing the people's trust.**

10. Epilogue: The Dawn of Awakening

Pakistan's democracy still walks in a long night.
But the meaning of night
is to teach people how to wait for light.

Fear is retreating,
and a new generation is rewriting the future.
Their words are no longer "obedience" and "patience,"
but "participation" and "responsibility."

When rulers finally understand
that sharing joy with the people
is nobler than sleeping with power,
that letting people speak
is far safer than silencing them—
then Pakistan will no longer be defined by fear,
but renamed by hope.

> **"Indeed, God does not change the condition of a people
> until they change what is in their hearts."**
> **— Qur'an 13:11**

This transformation has already begun
in countless awakened hearts.
And when each person chooses
to move from obedience to participation—
in that very moment,
democracy is born.

The Declaration of the Day of Return to the People
(For Freedom, Equality, and Justice)

Date: March 23
(Formerly Pakistan Day; now proclaimed as the "Day of Return to the People," symbolizing the true restoration of sovereignty to the citizens.)

Preface: The Final Deadline Set by God

God says:

> "He has made you successors (Khalifahs) upon the earth,
> to see which of you does good."
> — *Qur'an 6:165*

> **Power is not glory—it is a test.**
> **Every ruler is but a temporary trustee;**
> **every reign is a trial of the soul.**

Today, we proclaim:
the divine deadline has arrived.
This is not a deadline of politics,
but a deadline of conscience.

To all who still rule by fear,
who hide behind privilege and repression—
you must make a choice:

Will you continue to plunder, or choose repentance?
Will you cling to power through fear,
or return power through compassion?

For God also said:

> "Act justly; that is nearest to righteousness."
> — *Qur'an 5:8*

**To lay down the sword is not weakness;
to relinquish privilege is the truest courage.
When rulers return to conscience,
the people will answer with forgiveness,
history will remember with respect,
and God will pardon with mercy.**

Chapter I: The Return of the Citizens

We swear this day—
we will no longer live as subjects ruled by fear,
but as citizens standing with dignity.

To be a citizen means:
- Every person possesses the right to respect and to be heard.
- Governments exist to serve, not to dominate.
- Religion should inspire goodness, not justify violence.
- The wealthy should create through honesty, not sustain power through greed.
- Soldiers should protect the people, not threaten them.

This is the order ordained by God.

> **"Indeed, God does not change the condition of a people
> until they change what is in their hearts."**
> — *Qur'an 13:11*

Today, we choose to change our hearts.

Chapter II: A Call to the Rulers

In the name of faith, we call upon all rulers—
Lay down your weapons, and return to humanity.

This is your final chance for forgiveness,
and your only path to rebirth.

If you end your fear,
cease repression,
release imprisoned consciences,
and return power to the people—
you shall not be condemned, but honored.

But if you refuse to awaken,
if you continue to rule through lies and fear,
then history will judge you,
the people will reject you,
and God will abandon you.

For God has said:

> **"He does not love the unjust."**
> **— *Qur'an 3:57***

Chapter III: Equality and Joy with the People

Happiness does not come from plunder—it comes from sharing.
Safety does not come from suppression—it comes from trust.

A true leader is not one who sits upon a throne,
but one who kneels to walk beside the people.

When a ruler bows before the people,
it is not humiliation—it is liberation.
It is the moment when the soul sheds fear,
and history truly begins.

To share joy and equality with the people—
that is the root of happiness,
and the beginning of divine blessing.

Chapter IV: The Covenant of Justice

From this day forward,
every citizen, every community, every school,
every worker and every woman
is a signer of this covenant.

We will not seek justice through violence,
but defend dignity through conscience.
We will not answer oppression with hatred,
but confront lies with truth.

This covenant bears no military flag—
only the flame of faith and the fire of the human heart.

Chapter V: March 23 — The Day of Return to the People

March 23 is no longer merely a remembrance of the Republic.
It is the day the soul returns to justice.

On this day, we shall hold:
- Morning Prayers and Oaths: simultaneous gatherings in mosques and public squares across the nation.
- Voices of Truth Assemblies: where the silenced will tell the buried truths of history.
- Peace Actions: medical aid, education drives, and poverty relief—symbols of reconstruction.
- Candlelight Vigils: honoring the souls of those who died for justice.

Through nonviolent acts,
we will let the world hear the awakening of this land.

Chapter VI: The Will of God

God never strips humans of freedom;
He gives them the power to choose.
And today—that moment of choice has come.

The soul of this nation now stands
at the boundary between fear and awakening.
Those who choose fear will perish with darkness;
those who choose justice will walk with light.

This is the divine will:
that every person reclaim mastery of their own soul,
and that every nation learn once again
to govern itself by truth.

Chapter VII: The Oath of Freedom

Before God we swear:
we will not bow to fear,
we will not repay hatred with hatred.
In the name of justice,
we will rebuild a nation of freedom.

Let God bear witness—
this land shall no longer belong to violence and lies,
but to those who choose love, peace, and dignity.

> **"Act justly; that is nearest to righteousness."**
> *— Qur'an 5:8*

On March 23,
we will no longer commemorate the birth of a state,
but witness the rebirth of a soul.

Final Proclamation

This is the final divine deadline to all rulers:
Lay down your fear.
Lay down your privilege.
Lay down your sword.
Return power to the people,
and dignity to humanity.

Then—
you shall be remembered with honor in history,
find peace in this life,
and earn blessing in the next.

This is the will of God,
and the awakening of the people.

— The Declaration of the Day of Return to the People
March 23 — The Day the Light of the Republic Returns

Appendix: Civic Return Action Manual (90-Day Peaceful Awakening Plan)
— A Covenant for Justice, Freedom, and Faith —

Target Date: March 23 · Day of Return to the People

1) Core Vision

Pakistan's true republic
is not determined by armies, parties, or elites—
it is founded on the conscience of every citizen.

March 23 is not merely a national day;
it is a return of the soul—
the people reclaim the courage stolen by fear,
and those in power lay down hearts clouded by authority.

> **"Indeed, God does not change the condition of a people until they change what is in their hearts."**
> *— Qur'an 13:11*

2) Three-Phase Structure (90 Days)

Phase I: Awakening of Faith and Conscience (Days 1–30)

Theme: Break the silence, return to the heart.
- Pulpit Initiative:
On Friday (Jummah) gatherings in mosques and community centers, scholars preach on *Justice and Compassion*—with *Qur'an 5:8* ("Do justice; that is nearest to piety") as the core verse.
- Family Dialogue Day:
Encourage home discussions: *What is freedom? What is dignity?* Let kinship open cracks in the wall of social fear.
- School & University Forums:
Hold talks on *Citizenship and Faith*, inviting students to explore justice from ethical, nonpartisan angles.

- Social Media Campaign:

Hashtags: #ReturnToThePeople, #JusticeReturns, #FearToFaith.
Post one verse + one line of conscience daily to spark a nationwide online awakening.

Phase II: Truth and Union (Days 31–60)

Theme: Connect communities, unveil truth.
- "Light of Truth" Community Circles:

Open, non-confrontational dialogues in each city with religious leaders, educators, women representatives, and youth.
Theme: *"Our Pain, Our Responsibility."*
- Media & Arts Actions:

Encourage local artists, journalists, and students to produce short films, poetry, and paintings telling the journey *from fear to hope*.
- Charity & Public Service:

Launch Walk for the People: free clinics, clean-ups, scholarships—symbolizing *action instead of complaint*.
- Inter-Sect/Interfaith Week:

Joint prayers by different Islamic schools and minority faiths, affirming that justice belongs to all humanity, not a single sect.

Phase III: Oath of Peace and Justice (Days 61–90)

Theme: From conscience to action, from action to covenant.
- Form the "Civic Return Union":

Voluntary coalition of community groups, educators, religious leaders, labor unions, and youth.
Joint Statement:
"We will not govern by fear, nor be silenced by lies;
faith is our root, justice our path."
- Provincial "Nights of Justice Lights":

On Day 80, light candles nationwide—praying that truth will illuminate fear.
- Final Week (Mar 16–22):

Peace-pledge rallies in Lahore, Karachi, Islamabad, and Peshawar.

All activities must be nonviolent, lawful, and open to the media.
Oath (recited by religious and civic leaders):
"In the name of God, I lay down fear;
I take justice as my faith and compassion as my strength;
I am no longer a silent subject—
I am a citizen with dignity."

3) March 23 · Day of Return Ceremonies

Morning: Nationwide Prayers & Oath (in unison)
- Joint prayers in mosques, churches, and public squares; readings of:
  - *Qur'an 6:165* **(the trust of stewardship)**
  - *Qur'an 5:8* **(act justly)**
  - *Qur'an 13:11* **(self-change)**
- Local leaders, teachers, or physicians read the Declaration of Return to the People.

Midday: Community Action & Service Day
- "People-First" volunteer drives everywhere:
meals for the poor, free clinics, neighborhood cleanups, school repairs—
symbolizing that power should serve, not control.

Evening: Forum of Truth and Reconciliation
- "Night of Reconciliation" in city centers: ordinary citizens share stories of oppression and hope.
No accusations, no revenge—only truth and reform.

Night: Vigil and Rite of Light
- Ten thousand lights kindled—fear departing, faith reborn.
- Recitation:
"May the light of justice shine upon the land;
may God forgive the darkness of the past,
and let this nation be seen anew."

4) Code of Peace (Nonviolence Principles)

1.   **No response to provocation.**
Insults, violence, or disruptions are met with silence and prayer.
2.   No property damage.
Public order and respect come first.
3.   No hate speech.
Use only words like *truth, justice, mercy, people.*
4.   No sectarian or ethnic incitement.
This movement belongs to everyone, not to any faction.
5.   Protect women and children.
Provide safe zones, medical stations, and legal aid at gatherings.
6.   Transparency & accountability.
Publicly disclose all organizers and sources of funding.

5) International Friends and Observers

Invite international media, human-rights groups, and faith-peace representatives
as witnesses and recorders.
This is not an appeal for outside rescue, but a testimony to the world that—
faith and democracy can walk together;
compassion and justice can coexist.

6) Final Prayer

"Do justice; that is nearest to piety."
— *Qur'an 5:8*

Lord,
teach those in power to lay down fear and learn to serve;
teach the people to put down hatred and learn to participate;
let this land be bounded not by blood,
but by the light of truth.

May March 23 become our shared Day of Freedom;
may every person, in God's light,
rediscover their dignity.

— Civic Return Initiative
Islamabad · Lahore · Karachi
First Issued: March 23,

GB **Appeal for the Protection of Peaceful Citizens**

— A Message to All Institutions, Officials, and Believers

In the name of Allah, the Most Merciful, the Most Compassionate:

> **"Be just; that is nearer to righteousness."**
> **— *Qur'an 5:8***

Justice is not rebellion, and peace is not weakness.
They are the heart of faith and the foundation of any true nation.

Today, we speak with one voice:
No force, under any authority, shall harm peaceful citizens of Pakistan.

Our Principles

1. Life is sacred.
Every human life is a creation of God and must be protected.
2. Peace is an act of faith.
To harm one's own unarmed people is to betray both humanity and belief.
3. Law and conscience are one.
True loyalty lies with the Constitution and with justice, not with fear.
4. Accountability before God and history.
Those who act in compassion will be remembered;
those who act in cruelty will be judged.

Our Appeal

- Cease all violence against peaceful citizens.
- Protect the right to peaceful assembly and free speech.
- Ensure police and armed forces act under the rule of law.
- Encourage dialogue and reconciliation between all communities.

Our Pledge

We will remain peaceful, disciplined, and faithful.
We respect law, and we ask the law to respect us.
We honor the officers who protect us—
and remind them: you serve the people, not power.

> **"Indeed, Allah will not change the condition of a people
> until they change what is in themselves."**
> — *Qur'an 13:11*

Civic Return Initiative
Islamabad · Lahore · Karachi
March 23,

Chapter 7 – The Full Preparation for a True Democratic Transition

— The Vision of Peace, Future, and Equality in Every Human Heart —

I. Awakening Before Transformation

Every rebirth in history begins with a change in thought.

For decades, Pakistan has been trapped between two kinds of fear:
the fear of the powerful — of losing control,
and the fear of the poor — of losing survival.

But a true transformation
is not a revolution driven by anger,
it is a rebirth built upon conviction.

When the people begin to believe
that freedom is not chaos,
that equality is not a threat,
but the foundation of order and dignity—
that is the moment transformation begins.

II. True Democracy Is Not a Change of Faces, but a Change of Mindset

Democracy is not a ritual of voting;
it is a culture of accountability.

When citizens start asking:
"Where did this tax money go?"
"Is this policy just?"
"Is this official honest?"
then democracy is already being born—
in street conversations and daily dialogue.

A genuine democratic transition

does not wait for leaders to change;
it begins when everyone acts at once:

- Teachers foster critical thinking in classrooms;
- Journalists choose to speak the truth;
- Religious leaders preach compassion and justice;
- Businesspeople compete through integrity, not bribery;
- Citizens replace anger with reason in public debate;
- Law enforcers remember they serve people, not orders.

When every member of society reclaims their moral duty, power finally returns to institutions, not individuals.

III. The Three Conditions of Transformation

1 Truth — The Revelation
Without truth, there is no transformation.
All buried wounds — political persecution, corruption, social injustice —
must be confronted with honesty.
Only a nation brave enough to face its own wrongs
can rebuild a system grounded in justice.

2 Trust — The Reconstruction
Authoritarian rule destroys trust,
teaching people to doubt each other,
even to doubt goodness itself.
Yet true revival begins by learning to believe again:
to believe that law can protect,
that speech can change reality,
that honesty deserves respect.

3 Institution — The Safeguard
Freedom without institutions collapses into chaos.
Transparent courts, independent media,
autonomous local governments, and fair election commissions—
these are not ornaments of democracy;
they are its very foundation.

IV. The Nation Must First Be Born in the People's Hearts

Before democracy arrives in law,
it must first be born in every person's heart.

It is a vision of a country—
where homes are free from fear,
systems free from privilege,
classrooms free from lies,
and the poor are no longer forgotten.

A land where children can learn truth freely,
women can walk safely in the streets,
workers can live with dignity by their labor,
believers can pray side by side in mosques, churches, and temples,
and government exists only to serve the people.

Such a nation does not need new rulers—
it needs new citizens:
citizens of dignity,
citizens of conviction.

V. The Covenant Between Faith and Freedom

> **"Indeed, God commands justice and fairness."**
> — *Qur'an 16:90*

Faith and freedom are not opposites.
True faith demands the courage to face truth;
true freedom requires the discipline of justice.

The soul of democracy lies not in slogans on the streets,
but in the conscience of each individual.

When a person chooses honesty over lies,
understanding over hatred,
responsibility over indifference—

that person is already prepared for transformation.

VI. The Spiritual Map of Transformation

Stage	Goal	Representative Actions
1 Inner Awakening	From fear to conviction	Education reform, renewal of faith teachings
2 Civic Connection	From isolation to cooperation	Community dialogues, youth platforms, women's forums
3 Institutional Reconstruction	From rule by men to rule of law	Judicial independence, media transparency, local autonomy
4 Global Integration	From closure to openness	Educational exchange, fair trade, cultural trust

VII. The Path of Peaceful Transformation

Peaceful transformation is not the choice of the weak—
it is the most courageous revolution of all.

For it asks a nation
not to answer violence with hatred,
nor replace justice with revenge,
but to replace revenge with institutions,
and anger with the rule of law.

The truest warrior
is not the one who carries a weapon,
but the one who still believes in light
in the darkest hour of history.

VIII. Conclusion: A Covenant for the Future

Before God and before the people, we make this pledge—

We will guard justice through faith,
defend freedom with conscience,

rebuild reason through education,
and strengthen equality through institutions.

When this covenant takes root in every heart,
democratic transformation will no longer be a dream,
but a destiny.

Then, Pakistan will no longer be defined by fear—
but reborn through hope.

Chapter 8 – Rebuilding the System: Making the People the Foundation of the Nation

— From Towers of Power to Bridges of Trust —

I. The Collapsing Tower: The Illusion of the Old System

Authoritarian states often appear solid but are, in truth, fragile.
They build walls from fear and crown them with privilege—
beneath the walls lies silent oppression,
above them, the revelry of a few.

The fatal flaw of the old order is this:
it believes the state is born of power,
not founded upon trust.

When the law becomes the ruler's shield,
when the judiciary bows to command,
when the army forgets its mission to protect the people—
the tower begins to crumble.

And the starting point of reconstruction
must be trust.

II. The Foundation of Trust: Three Layers of Institutional Reconstruction

To rebuild a modern, just, and people-centered state,
we must reform at three interconnected levels:
political, judicial, and social institutions.

(1) Political System: Power Must Return to the People

Constitutional Reform and Popular Sovereignty

- Establish "sovereignty belongs to the people" as the supreme constitutional principle.
- Reform any clauses enabling military interference, privilege immunity, or religious exclusivity through constitutional amendment and national referendum.

2 Local Autonomy and Decentralization

- Delegate administrative and fiscal powers to provinces and cities.
- Build democracy from the community level, bringing decision-making closer to the people.
- Each region should have authority over its own budgets, education, healthcare, and infrastructure.

3 Parliamentary and Party Reform

- Create an independent election commission to ensure transparency and fairness.
- Limit political donations and require full public declaration of assets.
- Encourage youth, women, and workers to participate in politics—
to form a parliament that reflects the nation's true diversity.

4 The Military's Return to Its Constitutional Mission

- The army's sole duty is to defend national security and constitutional order, not to govern politics or the economy.
- Military budgets must be transparent and subject to parliamentary oversight.
- True honor lies not in control, but in courage—protecting the people.

(2) Judicial System: Making the Law a Refuge for All

1 Judicial Independence and Accountability

- Judges shall be appointed by an independent commission, free from political interference.

- Establish a *Citizen Legal Ombudsman* to oversee judicial conduct and receive complaints.

2 Equality Before the Law
- Abolish all legal discrimination based on class, gender, or religion.
- Implement a *Grassroots Legal Aid System* ensuring that even the poor have access to defense.

3 Transparent Trials and Media Oversight
- Judicial proceedings should be as open as possible, allowing society to supervise the practice of justice.

(3) Social System: From Fear to Dignity in Public Life

1 Educational Reform: Reason and Faith in Harmony
- Education should cultivate critical thinking, not blind obedience.
- Let moral education be guided by faith, and reason be built on science.
- Introduce universal compulsory education and free secondary schooling.

2 Healthcare and Social Protection: Centering Life
- Establish a *Universal Health Service* ensuring medical access for all.
- Provide a basic living guarantee for poor families—
so that dignity, not charity, becomes the foundation of society.

3 Freedom of the Press and Information Transparency
- Abolish censorship and protect whistleblowers and freedom of speech.
- The media must be the eyes of society, not the mouthpiece of power.

4 Protection for Women and the Vulnerable

- Enact and enforce laws against gender discrimination and domestic violence.
- Guarantee women equal rights in education, employment, and political participation.

III. The Spiritual Core of Institutional Reconstruction

**"Indeed, God commands justice and righteousness,
and that you show kindness to one another."**
— *Qur'an 16:90*

The roots of democracy are not in the text of the constitution,
but in the honesty of the human soul.

The strength of the rule of law lies not in punishment,
but in trust.

The purpose of rebuilding institutions
is not merely to divide power,
but to institutionalize conscience—
so that integrity is no longer a sacrifice,
and justice becomes the normal state of society.

IV. From Towers of Power to Bridges of Trust

Pakistan's future does not need a new "center of power,"
but a new structure of trust.

The builders of that bridge
will not be a few elites,
but every citizen willing to take part in public life.

This bridge will span the divides of wealth and poverty,
sect and class, language and region.
It will connect faith in Islam with the principles of modern governance,
link rural workers with urban innovators,

and join the wounds of the past to the hopes of the future.

V. Conclusion: A Nation of the People

A true nation is not sustained by power,
but held together by trust.

When the people trust the law,
when the government trusts its people,
when faith trusts freedom,
the nation becomes unshakable.

What we must build is not a new regime—
but a new civilization.

"The light of God is not in the palace, but in the human heart."

When each person begins to believe:
"I have a duty to make the world more just,"
"I have the power to help others live with dignity,"
then, at that very moment—
Pakistan will be reborn.

Chapter 9 – The People's Covenant: From Trust to an Age of Citizenship

— When the Nation No Longer Belongs to the Rulers, but to the People Themselves —

I. From Subjects to Citizens

For Pakistan to achieve true transformation,
a new identity must be born — the Citizen.

In the past, the people were defined as *those who obey.*
They struggled between command and fate.
But a new era requires that every person realize:
I am the owner of my nation.

The awakening of citizens is not a revolt of anger,
but a calm and steadfast conviction:
I have the *right* to question, and the *duty* to act;
I have the *freedom* to criticize, and the *responsibility* to uphold the law.

When the people's mindset shifts
from being "managed" to "co-governing,"
democracy ceases to be a ritual —
and becomes a way of daily life.

II. The Three Pillars of the People's Covenant

1 Transparency

In darkness, power decays.
In sunlight, truth grows.

Transparency is not a slogan — it is a system design:
- All budgets must be public.

- All government procurement must be traceable.
- All election results, candidates' assets, and policy debates must be fully open to the public.

Transparency is the beginning of trust,
and the safeguard that prevents democracy from deforming.

2 Accountability

Every public official is a servant of the people.
Anyone who betrays their oath, abuses authority,
or engages in corruption must face public scrutiny and legal justice.

Accountability is not merely punishing the corrupt —
it is teaching a society what honesty and dignity mean.

When the people no longer fear accountability,
but embrace it as an honor,
the nation moves from the order of fear
to the order of reason.

3 Participation

True democracy does not happen on election day,
but on every day thereafter.

Citizen participation means engaging
in schools, communities, media, and religious groups—
to discuss, monitor, and build together.

Local councils should welcome residents' input;
youth should help design and supervise policy;
religious leaders should guide believers
to take part in social affairs through peaceful means.

Participation turns citizens from spectators
into co-creators of the future.

III. The Union of Faith and Covenant

**"And fulfill the covenant, for indeed the covenant will be
questioned."**
— *Qur'an 17:34*

This verse reveals a profound truth:
The maturity of faith lies not in rituals of worship,
but in whether one keeps promises—
to others, to society, to truth itself.

The *People's Covenant* is not just a political document;
it is a spiritual vow:
- The citizen's honesty toward the state;
- The state's respect toward its citizens;
- Mutual trust and shared responsibility between them.

Only when faith and institutions unite
can democracy retain its soul,
and freedom avoid becoming chaos.

IV. The Mission of the Young Generation

Pakistan has one of the youngest populations in the world.
This is both a challenge and a promise.

This generation of youth
is no longer satisfied with slogans or hollow heroism.
They seek truth, dignity, and opportunity.

The birth of the civic era must begin with them:
- They are the bearers of the information revolution,
capable of breaking censorship and spreading truth.

- They are the pioneers of an innovative economy,
proving that creation and independence bring power.
- They are the seeds of future leadership,
learning rationality and empathy through public dialogue.

Empowering youth to speak and act
is the only way to prevent society from aging
and institutions from ossifying.

V. Women and Social Justice

Any democracy without women's participation
is incomplete.

Women are not the appendages of society —
they are its builders and its future.

From education and employment,
to property rights, legal protection,
political representation, and community leadership —
every reform must guarantee women equal participation.

> **"Men and women are protectors and allies of one another."**
> *— Qur'an 9:71*

> A society that respects women
> is one that respects the life created by God.

VI. The Power of Community: From Villages to Cities

The roots of civil society lie not in the capital,
but in the community.

When local people govern local affairs,
democracy becomes the most effective form of education.

Village elders, teachers, doctors, and youth volunteers
can all participate in local decisions—
from building schools to managing water,
from sanitation to safety.

In cities, community centers, unions, and associations
can provide platforms for training, dialogue, and oversight.

The strength of a nation
comes not from commands issued from above,
but from trust built from below.

VII. The Media as Guardians of Truth

The duty of the media is not to please power,
but to tell the truth to the people.

In a civic era, freedom of the press
is the immune system of the nation.
When media are silenced, rumors become viruses;
when media are free, truth becomes light.

Reforms should include:
- A *Public Media Fund* to ensure independence;
- A *Journalist Safety Law* to prevent violence and retaliation;
- A *Citizen Journalism System* to enable community oversight.

**Truth must cease to be a privilege for the brave,
and become a right shared by all.**

VIII. The International Responsibility of Civil Society

A mature democracy is also a conscious global citizen.
A truly free nation does not seek gain through hatred,
but earns respect through justice.

Civil society must become a force for regional peace—
taking part in refugee aid, environmental protection,
and educational cooperation.

Pakistan's future does not lie in isolated nationalism,
but in a shared responsibility of faith and civilization.

IX. Epilogue: The Light of the Covenant

"God gives justice as His light and mercy as His path."

The birth of a civic age
is not a miracle of institutions—
it is a revolution of the soul.

When every person is willing to keep promises,
to demand accountability,
and to participate with courage,
democracy no longer needs to be defended by slogans,
for it already lives in the people's hearts.

This is the new covenant:
The state returns to the people,
and the people rebuild the state.

Chapter 10 — The Rebirth of Civilization: A Nation of Faith and Humanity in Harmony

— *From the Age of Fear to a Civilization of Compassion*

I. The Century of Fear

Throughout the twentieth century, Pakistan was held hostage by two kinds of fear —
fear of war from without, and fear of tyranny from within.

Fear silenced the mouth and sealed the heart.
It turned religion into a political instrument,
and transformed pure faith into mere ritual obedience.

Thus, a nation rich in faith lost the soul of its faith to fear.

But God does not favor the fearful.
He favors the brave —
those who choose to illuminate darkness with truth and compassion.

> **"Do not be afraid; indeed, I am with you both."**
> **— *Qur'an 20:46***

II. The Renewal of Faith: From Fear of God to Love of God

Religion never called for blind submission.
It calls for honesty, mercy, and responsibility.

True faith is not the faith of those who fear punishment,
but of those who wish to embody goodness itself.

The rebirth of faith is the awakening of humanity.
When a Muslim ceases to ask, *"Who deserves punishment?"*
and begins to ask, *"Whom can I help?"*
the true meaning of Islam is reborn.

> "Indeed, God commands justice, kindness, and generosity to relatives."
> — *Qur'an 16:90*

III. The Return of Humanity: From System to Conscience

Democracy frees people from tyranny,
but humanity frees them from indifference.

Institutions can establish order,
but only compassion can create civilization.

A truly modern nation is not a pile of technology,
but a continuity of ethics.

A humane society is one where:
- The law protects the weakest;
- Healthcare is available to all, rich or poor;
- Education transcends sect and class;
- The media glorify truth, not power;
- Religions respect one another instead of attacking each other.

**Such a society is not utopia—
it is what emerges when faith and institutions mature together.**

IV. The Rebirth of Civilization: From Power to Compassion

Every great civilization began with the return of compassion.

The greatness of Egypt lay not in its pyramids,
but in the moment when pharaohs learned to revere life.
The glory of Persia was not in its palaces,
but in the Zoroastrian creed of "Good Thoughts, Good Words, Good Deeds."
The brilliance of Islam lay not in conquest,
but in the Prophet Muhammad's words:

"The strongest among you is the one who can control his anger."

When power learns restraint,
when rulers learn humility,
and when believers learn to listen—
that is when civilization is reborn.

V. The Sacred Mission of Education

Education is not the transfer of knowledge,
but the cultivation of the soul.

The education of the past taught memorization;
the education of the future must teach reflection.

Every child must be taught:
to respect difference, to seek truth,
to speak honestly, and to reject hatred.

Schools must become the seed fields of peace,
not factories of obedience.

> **"Seeking knowledge is the duty of every believer."**
> **— Prophet Muhammad**

> Knowledge is light, and light dispels ignorance—
> and ignorance is the soil where tyranny grows.

VI. The Restoration of Culture: Returning Art to the Soul

Civilization is not only architecture or economy;
it also needs poetry, music, and art.

Art is the mirror of a nation,
the warmth that reminds people what it means to be alive.

Poets, painters, musicians, filmmakers—
they are the healers of a nation's soul.

When Pakistan once again gives its youth
the space to create,
the nation will learn to breathe anew.

VII. A Nation of Peace: Faith and Reason Together

Peace is not a diplomatic tactic;
it is a philosophy of living.

A truly peaceful nation does not need to display power to the world;
it needs to display humanity.

It takes pride not in war,
but in its doctors, teachers, poets, and engineers.

When a nation's greatness no longer arises from victory in battle,
but from the goodness of its people—
then peace becomes its faith.

VIII. The Covenant with God: A New Order of Civilization

"He created all things through mercy,
and sustains the heavens and the earth through justice."

The ultimate goal of civilization
is not to be a powerful nation,
but a good nation.

The Kingdom of God is not in the heavens—
it is realized in human hearts.

When each person chooses kindness over fear,
truth over falsehood,

responsibility over escape,
that is the beginning of *God's kingdom on earth.*

IX. Epilogue: The Nation of Light

One day—
when the call to prayer from the mosque
and the bell of the school ring together;
when judges cite the mercy, not the wrath, of scripture;
when the youth take pride in creation, not hatred;
when women walk freely on the streets;
when the poor are no longer forgotten—

Then, Pakistan will no longer be a country on a map,
but a symbol of civilization.

A nation where
faith and reason thrive together,
compassion and justice coexist,
freedom and order sustain each other.

> **"The light of God shines over the heavens and the earth—
> not from oil, nor from fire,
> but from within the human heart."**
> — *Qur'an 24:35*

Afterword

This book is not an ending—
it is an invitation.

An invitation for every Pakistani
to build the nation within their own heart;
an invitation for every believer
to live out God's compassion in action;
an invitation for every leader, scholar, youth, and mother
to let civilization be reborn in daily life.

For the Pakistan of the future
will not be written by power,
but by the kindness of its people.

Digital Bureaucracy and the Mirage of Modernization: A Case Study of Pakistan's E-Visa System and the Search for Hope

Author: *ButterflyMan*
Independent Researcher & Entrepreneur

Abstract

This paper examines Pakistan's e-visa process as a microcosm of the country's deeper governance dilemma — a nation modernizing on the surface yet paralyzed by structural inertia beneath. Through firsthand experience, comparative economic data, and sociological analysis, the study reveals how excessive bureaucracy, elite capture, and military influence reflect a psychology of control rather than service. A comparative lens with Bangladesh and Indonesia demonstrates that technological progress without institutional trust creates only a digital mirage. The paper argues that genuine hope for Pakistan lies not in military-managed modernization but in civic trust, youth entrepreneurship, and moral governance capable of transforming control into competence.

Keywords: Pakistan, Bangladesh, e-visa, bureaucracy, governance, entrepreneurship, digital transformation, wages, elite capture, hope

1. Introduction: Encountering the Digital Wall

The Pakistani e-visa experience provides a revealing metaphor for the state itself. When applying online, one expects efficiency and openness; instead, one encounters an opaque labyrinth of forms, authenticator apps, and surprise fees. The system seems designed less to facilitate travelers than to remind them of the state's presence.

Each redundant verification step feels performative — as though the government seeks to prove its existence through inconvenience. This ritualistic complexity is not a technical glitch; it is the manifestation of a governance philosophy where visibility substitutes for efficiency and control replaces service.

2. Bureaucracy as Identity: The Colonial Inheritance

Pakistan inherited its bureaucratic DNA from British India. The colonial "file culture" — valuing signatures, stamps, and formality over outcomes — survives in digital form. The e-visa's endless steps mirror the same performative logic: the purpose is not to complete a process efficiently but to demonstrate authority.

Digitalization without institutional reform simply automates inefficiency. The nation's "Digital Pakistan" initiative remains trapped within bureaucratic self-preservation — producing data, not development. As Shad et al. (2012) note, cultural resistance and hierarchical mindsets undermine public-sector technology adoption, turning reform into ritual.

3. The Military Shadow and the Civilian Mask

Behind Pakistan's bureaucratic front lies a political reality: the military's enduring dominance. Since the 1958 coup, no civilian administration has governed without its shadow. The state functions as a security apparatus first and a service provider second.

In such a system, even an e-visa becomes a security checkpoint — not an invitation. Repeated authentications and data collection reflect the logic of surveillance, not service. Civilian ministries act as façades for deeper, unaccountable power structures. Transparency International and the Middle East Institute (2025) both describe this as a "hybrid regime": formally democratic, functionally military.

4. Economic Oligarchy: One Hundred Families and a Captured State

Pakistan's economy is dominated by an alliance of elites — roughly one hundred families, supported by military and bureaucratic networks, controlling key industries, banks, and land holdings. This "feudal-corporate model" leaves little space for social mobility or competition.

The result is stagnation masked as stability. Economic policy, investment access, and even industrial licenses remain instruments of patronage. In contrast, Bangladesh's rise over the past two decades reflects the opposite trajectory: decentralization, inclusion, and small-scale enterprise.

4.1 Macroeconomic Divergence: Bangladesh and Pakistan (2005–2025)

Year	Bangladesh GDP (US$ B)	Pakistan GDP (US$ B)	GDP per capita (US$) – Bangladesh	GDP per capita (US$) – Pakistan
2005	75 B	125 B	550	890
2010	120 B	180 B	780	1,100
2015	200 B	275 B	1,240	1,440
2020	340 B	270 B	2,020	1,320
2023	437 B	375 B	2,650	1,560
2025 (IMF est.)	450 B	410 B	2,730	

(Sources: World Bank 2024; IMF WEO 2025)

In 2005, Pakistan's economy was 70% larger than Bangladesh's. Two decades later, Bangladesh leads in both total and per-capita GDP. Its manufacturing exports, female labor participation, and consistent policy reforms have delivered compound growth of nearly 6–7% annually. Pakistan, constrained by political volatility, elite capture, and energy crises, has seen cycles of inflation and stagnation.

Where Bangladesh invested in industrial inclusion, Pakistan preserved industrial hierarchy.

4.2 The Rise of the "New Normal": Entrepreneurship and Social Mobility

Bangladesh's most profound transformation lies not in its GDP figures but in its entrepreneurial demography. Over the past 25 years, a wave of first-generation entrepreneurs — many under 35 — have entered the garment, tech, and service sectors. Programs such as *Startup Bangladesh Ltd.* and widespread access to micro-finance created an environment where ambition could translate into enterprise.

By contrast, Pakistan's economy remains sealed within its patronage networks. Military foundations, state-owned banks, and dynastic conglomerates dominate industry. Young Pakistanis seldom become factory owners; they become employees or emigrants. The country's economic imagination is still mediated by hierarchy.

This difference reveals why Bangladesh's growth is diffusive — generated by thousands of small firms — while Pakistan's remains concentrated, dependent on a few. As Kaushik Basu (2022) observed, development thrives when "many hands build the future, not when few hold the gate."

5. The Digital Mirage: Modernization Without Modernity

The e-visa experience encapsulates a broader pattern: technology implemented without institutional trust. While Pakistan's e-visa demanded redundant verification and hidden fees, Indonesia's system issued approval within ten minutes — simple, clear, automatic.

The difference is philosophical, not technological. Indonesia designs for trust until proven otherwise; Pakistan designs for suspicion until proven safe. Thus, both nations use digital tools, but only one achieves digital governance.

UN E-Government Survey (2022) ranks Pakistan 161st of 193 countries in service efficiency. Digital portals that should symbolize openness instead reinforce hierarchy — a virtual reproduction of bureaucratic fear.

6. Poverty, Pride, and Paradox

Poverty and pride coexist in Pakistan. Streets lined with underpaid workers stand beneath billboards celebrating "Vision 2025." Bureaucratic pride replaces institutional competence.

The factory floor reveals this contradiction most starkly.

6.1 Factory Wages and Living Reality (2013–2024)

Year	Bangladesh Avg. Wage (US$/month)	Pakistan Avg. Wage (US$/month)
2013	100 – 110	130 – 150
2016	130 – 150	160 – 170
2019	170 – 180	175 – 190
2022	210 – 230	180 – 200
2024	240 – 260	190 – 210

(Sources: ILO Wage Report 2024; World Bank Labor Dataset)

Despite beginning at lower wages, Bangladesh's factory workers now earn more in nominal terms and substantially more in purchasing power, thanks to export growth and stable currency policy. In Pakistan, chronic inflation and weak productivity have kept real wages stagnant.

The divergence between Dhaka's rising garment districts and Pakistan's declining textile hubs is symbolic: one built opportunity through simplification; the other suffocated it through control.

7. Where Is the Hope?

Hope persists, but it lies outside the bureaucracy — within Pakistan's people.

7.1 Youth and Civil Society

With over 60% of its population under 30, Pakistan stands on the threshold of either renewal or rupture. Young Pakistanis exposed to global comparisons understand that efficiency is not Westernization; it is civilization. Their frustration with red tape is not rebellion but realism.

Grass-roots educational initiatives like *The Citizens Foundation* and university incubators in Lahore and Karachi are nurturing small but transformative civic competencies — the first stirrings of a trust-based culture.

7.2 Women and Moral Modernization

Women's participation remains Pakistan's most underutilized force. Yet wherever women manage classrooms, local health programs, or small factories, efficiency rises. The moral modernization of governance will depend on integrating empathy — a traditionally "feminine" value — into public administration.

7.3 Learning from Bangladesh's Entrepreneurs

Bangladesh's "new normal" of young entrepreneurs offers a blueprint. Its success demonstrates that governance need not be perfect for progress to begin — it only needs to stop obstructing initiative. If Pakistan's state simply steps aside, its citizens will build what the bureaucracy cannot.

7.4 A Return to the People: The Hope of a Civilian Future

The ultimate hope for Pakistan lies in a peaceful realignment of power — when the military establishment, having long defined itself as the guardian of national stability, finally recognizes that true stability grows only from legitimacy.

If the military were to relinquish its grip on political and economic control, and allow the people to govern through transparent, free and fair elections, the entire structure of trust could begin to heal. Civilian institutions would regain both moral and functional authority; entrepreneurs, educators, and professionals could act without fear of arbitrary interference.

Such a transformation would not weaken the state — it would redeem it. The armed forces would return to their constitutional duty of defense, while the republic could finally focus on human development, education, and prosperity.

History suggests that nations rise not when their generals command politics, but when their citizens command their own future. Pakistan's most profound act of modernization will not be the next dam, missile, or e-government app, but the simple, radical act of restoring power to the people.

8. Conclusion: Between the System and the Soul

The e-visa that took days to arrive is more than a travel inconvenience — it is a mirror. It reflects a state where procedure has replaced purpose, and suspicion has replaced service.

Yet within Pakistan's confusion lies immense potential. Its youth are educated, connected, and restless; its entrepreneurs are inventive even under constraint; its people are proud not of privilege but of endurance.

If Bangladesh's trajectory shows anything, it is that reform begins the moment a government decides to trust its citizens.
Pakistan's future depends not on another "Vision 2025" plan but on a moral modernization — replacing control with competence, and fear with faith.

Only when a visa, a permit, or a factory license becomes a matter of service rather than suspicion will Pakistan rediscover its soul.

References

Alavi, H. (1972). *The State in Post-Colonial Societies: Pakistan and Bangladesh.* New Left Review, 74, 59–81.

Asian Development Bank. (2023). *Pakistan Country Gender Assessment Update 2023.* ADB Publications.

Basu, K. (2022). *Diffused Development: Reflections on Emergent Asia.* Oxford University Press.

Brookings Institution. (2024). *Pakistan's Democracy, its Military, and America.*

Castells, M. (2012). *Networks of Outrage and Hope.* Polity Press.

Hull, M. (2012). *Government of Paper: The Materiality of Bureaucracy in Urban Pakistan.* University of California Press.

International Labour Organization. (2024). *Global Wage Report 2024/25.*

Kaura, V. (2025). *Pakistan's Enduring Civil-Military Imbalance.* Middle East Institute.

Klitgaard, R. (2013). *Ideas for Pakistan: Governance and Growth.* Claremont Graduate University.

Shad, R., Chen, J. Q., Malik, A., & Azeem, M. F. (2012). ERP Implementation in Public Sector Organizations of Pakistan. *arXiv preprint arXiv:1207.2860.*

Transparency International. (2024). *Corruption Perceptions Index 2024.* Berlin.

United Nations. (2022). *E-Government Survey 2022.* UN DESA.

United States Institute of Peace. (2023). *Elite Capture and Development in Pakistan.* Washington DC.

World Bank. (2024). *World Development Indicators: Pakistan and Bangladesh Comparative Dataset.* Washington DC.

World Economic Outlook (IMF). (2025). *Country Profiles: Pakistan and Bangladesh.*

Appendix 1:

The Mirage of Iron Brotherhood: Authoritarian Alliances and the Absence of Public Legitimacy in Modernization

The Mirage of Iron Brotherhood: Authoritarian Alliances and the Absence of Public Legitimacy in Modernization

ButterflyMan
Independent Researcher based in New York
October 2025

Abstract

This article draws on the author's five-day field experience in Lahore, Pakistan, to reveal the human costs and institutional illusions behind so-called authoritarian "cooperation."
What is publicly framed as an "iron brotherhood" rests not on trust and popular consent but on fear, surveillance, and control.
Through first-hand observation and a concrete episode in which the author's passport was forcibly taken by military personnel on a public road, the paper shows how the logic of militarized governance and securitized friendship corrodes social trust, isolates foreign workers from local society, and turns modernization into spectacle.

The argument advances a moral and institutional claim: no alliance that excludes the people can be durable. Sustainable security and genuine friendship require human rights, transparency, and civic participation.
The article closes with a warning to authoritarian governments—particularly those that seek geopolitical loyalty through debt and armed protection—that fear cannot found legitimacy, and that faith in citizens is the only path to a humane modernity.

Keywords: authoritarian cooperation · China–Pakistan relations · modernization · militarization · human rights · trust crisis

Chapter M1 – Introduction: The Myth of the Iron Brotherhood

Across the last decade, "iron brotherhood" has become a diplomatic mantra across parts of Asia and Africa.

In press conferences and summits, it is presented as a civilizational bond— "a community of shared destiny" that promises new solidarity and hope among developing nations.

Yet the myth dissolves on contact with everyday life.

When I arrived as a researcher, airport halls were sparse, streets subdued, and foreign faces rare.

I was stopped for additional screening at the airport exit even after clearing procedures.

Only when a factory representative rushed over to explain—"foreigners, especially Chinese, cannot move about alone; special protection is required"—did I understand the grammar of this friendship.

What is advertised as fraternity is practiced as vigilance.

A friendship that needs guns for escort is not friendship but dependency.

This paper therefore examines how authoritarian alliances mask structural inequalities and manufacture the illusion of security and development in the absence of public legitimacy.

Chapter M2 – Five Days in Lahore: The Boundaries of Friendship

I spent five days in Lahore.

The city was energetic yet worn, dusty yet warm with humanity.

I visited eight factories—textiles, leather, garments—each led by people who were diligent, honest, and hospitable.

They spoke about inflation, power outages, and how the young dream of leaving; no one spoke about politics.

Throughout the trip I saw almost no Chinese presence in public:

no merchants in markets, no engineers walking freely, no familiar signage in hotels.

A driver told me, "Chinese cannot go out alone; they must have security."

Why? "It's the rule."

That sentence—"it's the rule"—is the portrait of an authoritarian system.

Rules do not arise from law but from habits enforced by power.

Security becomes the extension of fear; cooperation becomes a closed alliance.

A factory owner sighed that Belt and Road money never reached ordinary people and that the state still relied on IMF loans.

He was not angry—he was tired.

In such a society, numbness is more common than anger; anger requires hope, and they have learned to live without it.

Chapter M3 – Fear in the Night: The Passport Incident

At 1:00 a.m. on my fifth day, I took a taxi to catch a 4:00 a.m. flight.

The city along Aziz Bhatti Road was silent and broad.

A soldier raised his rifle and signaled us to stop.

I opened my passport and showed it through the window but refused to hand it over.

After a short exchange he walked away.

Moments later a man who appeared to be an officer approached, demanded to see the passport, and—without consent—took it directly from my hand.

The driver whispered that the road ahead was a military zone and foreigners could not pass.

We were forced to make a U-turn and detour to another side of the checkpoint.

The passport was not returned to me directly; it was given to the driver, from whom I retrieved it.

Fifteen minutes of detour felt like a small collapse of civilization.

If this is how soldiers treat a foreign visitor, how do they treat their own citizens?

Chapter M4 – From Personal Experience to Institutional Reflection

Two Pakistans emerged before me: a gentle, kind people—and a rigid, cold system sustained by fear.

The officer who seized my passport was not a singular villain but the product of a structure where power is a reflex.

In such a setting, taking a passport, forcing detours, and refusing explanation cease to be abuses and become "routine management."

This is institutionalized, unconscious violence.

Its root is not poverty but the long predominance of the military within the state.

The army reaches beyond defense into the economy, media, education, and the courts.

It is guardian and arbiter, executor and beneficiary.

Government becomes an extension of military power; society is trained for compliance.

Friendship and cooperation become covers for a civil–military bargain.

External assistance is folded into a security logic: every project becomes a "security project," every foreigner a "risk object."

Security displaces trust, prevention replaces exchange, and "development" becomes the repackaging of fear.

Chapter M5 – China's Mirror: The Illusion of Brotherhood

"If brothers require armed escort, can it still be called brotherhood?"

The relationship between China and Pakistan is promoted as the strongest of communities of destiny.
In practice, Chinese projects are militarized, Chinese workers are isolated, and local communities are kept outside the perimeter.
This is not equality or mutual understanding but a regime-to-regime insurance scheme.

As Basu (2022) observes, in many authoritarian settings development substitutes control for integration.
The result is surface-level prosperity without social trust.
For Beijing, this is a political gamble: buying loyalty with capital and hush with infrastructure.
Such loyalty collapses the moment fear loosens.

For Chinese citizens, this is a mirror: when we suppress the freedom of others in the name of national honor, we replay our own tragedy.

Chapter M6 – A Warning to Pakistan's Military

Pakistan's core crisis is not poverty but fear.

The arrogance of arms has seeped into every layer of life.

The army does not only guard the nation; it controls it.

It does not only defend security; it defines it.

It does not only execute orders; it manufactures them.

To the generals I say: fear is not order; weapons are not dignity.

You may preserve a surface calm, but you cannot arrest the course of history.

When soldiers stand above the law, when citizens fear their own military, and when government cannot restrain armed power, the nation has lost its soul.

True security arises from public trust; true honor from institutional self-restraint.

Chapter M7 – Return to Humanity and Rights

The foundation of modernity is not GDP curves or megaprojects but the restoration of humanity and rights.

A society that needs its army to protect friendship has already lost trust.

A state that maintains order through repression has already lost legitimacy.

The future of China–Pakistan relations must return to a civic foundation: respect free choice, recognize popular sovereignty as the only source of legitimacy, and bind power to law rather than law to power.

To all autocrats, a final warning: the only safe path is to lay down power and become ordinary citizens.

Conclusion – The Collapse of a Fear-Based Alliance

That night in Lahore, when my passport was taken, it was not only a document at stake but human dignity itself.

The myth of iron brotherhood conceals dependence on fear and the suppression of freedom.

History has never been kind to states that point guns at their people.

As my plane lifted into the night, one sentence remained:

"Fear ends where faith begins. The people will ultimately reclaim their power."

Author Note

ButterflyMan is an independent researcher and writer based in New York.
His work focuses on political transformation, human rights, and the moral
reconstruction of post-authoritarian societies.
He combines field observation with philosophical analysis to propose a path
toward humane, transparent, and law-bound modernization.

References

Basu, K. (2022). Diffused Development: Reflections on Emergent Asia. Oxford University Press.

Buzan, B., Wæver, O., & de Wilde, J. (1998). Security: A New Framework for Analysis. Lynne Rienner Publishers.

Diamond, L. (2021). Ill Winds: Saving Democracy from Russian Rage, Chinese Ambition, and American Complacency. Penguin.

Evans, P. (1995). Embedded Autonomy: States and Industrial Transformation. Princeton University Press.

Foucault, M. (1978). The History of Sexuality, Vol. 1. Pantheon Books.

Hull, M. S. (2012). Government of Paper: The Materiality of Bureaucracy in Urban Pakistan. University of California Press.

Levitsky, S., & Way, L. A. (2010). Competitive Authoritarianism: Hybrid Regimes after the Cold War. Cambridge University Press.

Rolland, N. (2019). China's Eurasian Century? Political and Strategic Implications of the Belt and Road Initiative. National Bureau of Asian Research.

Siddiqa, A. (2023). Military Inc.: Inside Pakistan's Military Economy. Pluto Press.

Slater, D. (2013). Ordering Power: Contentious Politics and Authoritarian Leviathans in Southeast Asia. Cambridge University Press.

Transparency International. (2024). Corruption Perceptions Index 2024. Transparency International.

Appendix 2:

China–Pakistan Relations Special Issue

"China–Pakistan Relations Special Issue"

"The Mirage of Iron Brotherhood": Authoritarian Alliances and the Absence of Public Legitimacy in Modernization

Author: ButterflyMan

Independent Researcher, U.S. Citizen of Chinese Origin

New York, 2025

Prologue: A Shock at the Airport

For many years, I have traveled among countries in Asia, Africa, and the Middle East.
Whether on the plateaus of Central Asia, in the ports of Southeast Asia, or in the industrial zones of Africa, one can see Chinese merchants, engineers, and builders everywhere—moving between cities and villages as symbols of a "globalized China."

Yet when I arrived in another country promoted as "China's closest brother," I encountered something unexpected.

At the airport exit, a police officer suddenly stopped me and asked to see my passport again.
I told him I was a U.S. citizen and had completed all the entry procedures.
He still insisted on checking it.

Soon the representative from a local factory who had come to meet me arrived and explained, in fluent English:

"Sir, Chinese nationals cannot move around here on their own. They must have special protection."

I froze.
It was the first time I realized that so-called "brotherhood" required "special protection" in order to function.
I presented my American passport, and only then did the officer let me pass.

This was my first visit to the country.
Until then, all I had heard were public narratives of "deep friendship": shared faith, shared cooperation, a shared future.
But this encounter shocked me—
if the friendship is genuine, why must a Chinese face rely on police escort simply to walk?

At that moment, I understood:
this "iron friendship" may indeed be iron—cold rather than warm.

Abstract

This paper examines the paradox of "authoritarian friendship" in parts of Asia and Africa, where nations bound by official rhetoric of solidarity and "brotherhood" rely on mutual control rather than mutual trust. Based on the author's firsthand field experiences as a U.S. citizen of Chinese origin traveling through these regions, the study reveals how a rhetoric of alliance masks a deeper insecurity: cooperation between authoritarian regimes creates security partnerships instead of social partnerships.

Using qualitative observation, political economy analysis, and sociological reflection, the paper argues that when diplomacy is monopolized by military elites and political patrons—while ordinary citizens are excluded—friendship becomes a state project sustained by surveillance, protection, and propaganda.

Empirical examples from multiple regions in Asia and Africa illustrate how large-scale infrastructure projects, "special protection systems," and debt-driven development reproduce inequality and fear. The paper concludes that without democratization, transparency, and public legitimacy, the so-called "iron brotherhood" between authoritarian partners remains an illusion—a political alliance forged in fear, not faith.

Keywords: Authoritarian alliance, political legitimacy, development myth, securitization, elite capture, fear politics, Asia, Africa

Chapter S1: Introduction — The Myth of the Iron Brotherhood

Over the past decade, "iron-like friendship" has become a diplomatic slogan among several countries in Asia and Africa.

In summits, cooperation agreements, and media reports, this relationship is depicted as a "community of shared destiny across mountains and seas," seemingly symbolizing new unity and hope among developing nations.

However, when one actually enters these societies, a different reality appears.

Airport security checkpoints, urban exclusion zones, and cordons around project sites—

the "scenes of friendship" are saturated with tension and vigilance.

Foreign engineers and investors are arranged to travel within closed compounds;

local residents watch from outside the "cooperation zones";

senior officials sign agreements in the name of "brotherhood,"

while ordinary people know almost nothing about these grand plans.

This is a typical model of authoritarian cooperation:

it is built on *mutual confidence between regimes*, not *trust between peoples*;

it relies on *military protection and security control*, not *social integration and cultural understanding*.

This structural contradiction constitutes a microcosm of the "modernization dilemma" in parts of contemporary Asia and Africa.

On the surface, roads are being built, ports are being dredged, and power grids are being extended;

but at a deeper level, the same logic of rule is being replicated:

control replaces service, obedience supplants thought, and fear maintains order.

Chapter S2 — Literature Review and Theoretical Framework

2.1. Authoritarian Mutual Assistance: The International Extension of Fear Politics

In research since the late Cold War, scholars have focused on a distinct form of international cooperation—mutual-assistance networks among authoritarian regimes. These states often form communities of interest around ideology, regime stability, and resistance to Western pressure.

Levitsky and Way (2010), in *Competitive Authoritarianism*, argue that authoritarian states "outsource legitimacy" through financial aid, security cooperation, and diplomatic cover, forming an informal support system.

Slater (2013) further notes that Southeast Asia's "ordering powers" rely on a "mutual fear equilibrium": domestically maintaining stability through control of the populace, and internationally avoiding isolation via alliances.

This authoritarian cooperation is not built on trust but on a coalition of fear. The parties fear democratic diffusion and external scrutiny, and therefore sustain power by mutually endorsing one another.

Diamond (2021) calls this the globalization of autocracy, observing that twenty-first-century authoritarian states are forming cross-regional alliances to resist liberal norms and mechanisms of accountability.

Across Asia, Africa, and the Middle East, this mutual assistance often appears as "national security cooperation," "counterterrorism partnerships," or "development partners."

On the surface these are economic and security collaborations; in essence they are exchanges of political legitimacy and repression technologies.

For example, a country's military might provide armed protection for foreign investment, while the investor secures political influence through loans and infrastructure.

This appearance of cooperation masks the systemic exclusion of people's participatory rights.

2.2. The Developmental State and the Trap of Modernization

The "developmental state" theory (Johnson, 1982) originally explained the industrial successes of Japan and South Korea, but in postcolonial contexts it often mutates into a state-led dependency structure.

Evans (1995), in *Embedded Autonomy*, argues that the key to a developmental state lies in "embedded autonomy"—the state must be capable of independent decision-making while remaining socially intertwined.

In most authoritarian systems, however, the state loses social embeddedness and retains only an isolated bureaucratic autonomy. The result is development reduced to performance projects and symbolic modernization.

Basu (2022) terms this phenomenon diffused development: economic growth figures become symbols of political legitimacy while livelihoods, education, and rights reforms are marginalized.

He notes that many postcolonial states fall into a developmentalist illusion—

building highways and ports without building trust and institutions.

This "developmentalism–authoritarianism" coupling is particularly evident in parts of Central Asia, Southeast Asia, and Africa.

Foreign-funded projects are packaged as a "community of shared destiny," yet governance becomes highly centralized.

Public works become stages for power display rather than products of a social contract.

Rolland (2019), in her study of the Belt and Road Initiative, points out that when infrastructure exports lack political transparency and social consultation, they easily morph into debt politics and even new forms of neo-colonial dependency.

2.3. Securitized Friendship: When Cooperation Is Hijacked by Military Logic

The concept of securitization originates from the Copenhagen School of security studies.

Buzan et al. (1998) argue that once an issue is defined as a "national security threat," it is removed from public debate and monopolized by the state apparatus.

In authoritarian diplomacy, this logic becomes pronounced: *friendship* is securitized; *cooperation* is militarized.

In parts of Asia and Africa, this "securitized friendship" manifests in the following ways:

1.   Large investment projects are classified as "strategic secrets," beyond public oversight;

2.   Foreign technicians and workers are guarded by the military, with minimal social contact;

3.   Once an attack or incident occurs, governments strengthen surveillance under the pretext of "external enemies" or "terrorism."

Thus, "friendship" is no longer a relationship between peoples but a form of **risk management defined by the security sector.**

Siddiqa (2023) notes that in a military-dominated economy, the security apparatus becomes the true economic intermediary—controlling contracts, protection, and land allocation—subsuming "development" under military jurisdiction.

The dangers of this model include:

- Trust yields to fear;

- "External friendship" becomes a pretext for internal repression;

- International cooperation is transformed into an extension of domestic domination.

The result is paradoxical: the more "friendly" the cooperation, the more armed protection it requires; the more "brotherhood" is emphasized, the greater the social distance becomes.

2.4. Elite Capture and Institutional Imbalance: Economic Consequences of Power Monopoly

From a political-economy perspective, elite capture is a key variable explaining the failure of development projects.

Klitgaard (2013) argues that in institutional environments characterized by resource scarcity and information opacity, powerholders tend to convert public resources into private gains.

Data from Transparency International (2024) show that most authoritarian countries remain in the lower tiers of corruption indices, and their outward cooperation projects carry significantly higher risk premiums compared to democracies.

This structural capture appears in international cooperation as:

- Non-transparent investment contracts;

- Project approvals concentrated in the hands of a few political figures;

- Profits flowing to transnational conglomerates and domestic oligarchs.

Barkan (2019), studying African development funds, notes that many aid programs are ultimately "absorbed upward"—that is, funds flow back to decision-making elites, while grassroots communities bear the costs of debt and environmental damage.

Within such systems, "iron brotherhood" rhetoric is used to mask distributive injustice.

Foreign capital becomes an extension of regime legitimacy rather than a source of public benefit.

As a result, economic cooperation loses its social foundation and development sinks into a self-reinforcing power loop.

2.5. Cultural and Discursive Reproduction: From Propaganda to Alienated Belief

Language is not merely a tool of communication; it is an extension of power.

Foucault (1978) argues that discourse shapes how people understand reality and delineates what can be said.

In the context of authoritarian cooperation, terms like "brotherhood," "community of shared destiny," and "mutual trust and mutual benefit" form a political-symbolic system that is both an ideological wrapper and a device of emotional governance.

Through repetition, the media constructs an inevitability of cooperation.

Citizens who question the relationship are labeled "disloyal" or "hostile."

Hull (2012), in his study of South Asian bureaucratic document culture, notes that the process of documentation itself becomes a symbol of rule—the state proves its existence through forms, approvals, and stamps rather than by improving people's lives.

Likewise, "cooperation documents," "memoranda of friendship," and "joint statements" symbolically represent development while substantively reinforcing a bureaucratic fraternity among states.

The hollowness of this language deprives international cooperation of human warmth.

2.6. Analytical Framework: From Structural Mutualism to Institutional Mirage

Synthesizing the literature yields a three-dimensional analytical framework:

Dimension: Power Mutualism

  •   Core Mechanism: Military–political elites sustain regime stability through security cooperation

  •   Key Sources: Levitsky & Way (2010); Slater (2013)

- Observed Outcomes: Securitized diplomacy; social exclusion

Dimension: Development Illusion

- Core Mechanism: Authoritarian systems use engineering and debt to fabricate an image of modernization

  - Key Sources: Basu (2022); Rolland (2019)

  - Observed Outcomes: Statistical growth with stagnant livelihoods

Dimension: Discursive Control

- Core Mechanism: States deploy language and media to construct false unity

  - Key Sources: Foucault (1978); Hull (2012)

  - Observed Outcomes: Symbolic cohesion; erosion of moral legitimacy

This framework reveals that the so-called "iron brotherhood" is not a genuine social bond but an institutional mirage.

Within this mirage, cooperation is defined as a security mission, development is reduced to a political symbol, and "the people" are demoted to mere spectators.

Accordingly, this study takes securitized friendship as the core analytical lens to examine how authoritarian regimes reproduce their internal logic of rule in cross-border cooperation—and to explore why, in the absence of democratic participation and institutional trust, these "brotherly alliances" are difficult to sustain.

References

Barkan, J. (2019). Aid and the Capture of Power in Africa. *African Studies Review*, 62(4), 601–624.

Basu, K. (2022). *Diffused Development: Reflections on Emergent Asia*. Oxford University Press.

Buzan, B., Wæver, O., & de Wilde, J. (1998). *Security: A New Framework for Analysis*. Lynne Rienner Publishers.

Diamond, L. (2021). *Ill Winds: Saving Democracy from Russian Rage, Chinese Ambition, and American Complacency*. Penguin.

Evans, P. (1995). *Embedded Autonomy: States and Industrial Transformation*. Princeton University Press.

Foucault, M. (1978). *The History of Sexuality, Vol. 1: An Introduction*. Pantheon Books.

Hull, M. (2012). *Government of Paper: The Materiality of Bureaucracy in Urban Pakistan*. University of California Press.

Johnson, C. (1982). *MITI and the Japanese Miracle*. Stanford University Press.

Klitgaard, R. (2013). *Ideas for Pakistan: Governance and Growth*. Claremont Graduate University.

Levitsky, S., & Way, L. A. (2010). *Competitive Authoritarianism: Hybrid Regimes after the Cold War*. Cambridge University Press.

Rolland, N. (2019). *China's Eurasian Century? Political and Strategic Implications of the Belt and Road Initiative*. NBR Press.

Siddiqa, A. (2023). *Military Inc.: Inside Pakistan's Military Economy (Updated Edition)*. Pluto Press.

Slater, D. (2013). *Ordering Power: Contentious Politics and Authoritarian Leviathans in Southeast Asia*. Cambridge University Press.

Transparency International. (2024). *Corruption Perceptions Index 2024*. Berlin: TI Secretariat.

Chapter S3 — Power Mechanisms and the Operational Logic of Securitized Friendship

3.1 Military–Political Structures: The Real Protagonists of Inter-State "Brotherhood"

In most authoritarian alliances among developing countries, the surface diplomacy of friendship conceals a deeper fact:
"state-to-state relations" are, in practice, relations between the military and political elites.

This structural feature is strikingly similar across parts of Asia, Africa, and the Middle East. The armed forces are not merely a defense institution; they sit at the core of national politics and act as managers of the economy.
As Siddiqa (2023) notes, in many postcolonial states the military commands its own business networks, real-estate holdings, and banking systems; its political role extends far beyond defense, forming a parallel state.

This parallel-state model produces two consequences:
First, national-security logics permeate all public policy, including foreign cooperation;
Second, the military becomes the de facto gatekeeper of international investment and infrastructure projects.

Thus, when foreign capital arrives, the real interlocutors are often not elected governments or independent agencies but military representatives or military-aligned conglomerates.
This structure "securitizes" external cooperation: project approvals, construction, and protection are placed under military control. In political-economy terms, this is militarized economic governance.

It also explains why, in some "brotherly" countries, the movements of foreign firms or technical staff are tightly restricted:

"Security" is not only to protect them; it is to ensure social separation and prevent civic contact. In other words, "protection" is itself an extension of rule.

3.2 Bureaucracy and Closed-Loop Development: The Rule of Documents

Such securitized governance typically pairs with another institutional trait—bureaucratic closure.

Hull (2012), in his study of South Asian bureaucratic culture, advances the idea of "file politics": documents exist not to serve the public but to prove power to itself. In authoritarian alliances, this logic is further institutionalized.

Examples include:

- Every investment must pass layers of approvals and security clearances;
- Entry permits for "cooperation zones" are more complex than diplomatic visas;
- Agencies duplicate approvals and deflect responsibility;
- Data and contracts are classified as "state secrets."

The stated rationale is "security and stability," but the substance is a performance of bureaucratic authority.

Each procedural layer is a reminder that the state machine holds absolute control.

Levitsky and Way (2010) note that competitive authoritarian regimes maintain a veneer of legality through procedural complexity—creating the *feeling* of institutions while closing scrutiny at decisive junctures.

The result: development projects appear orderly yet are inefficient, expensive, and unaccountable.

This bureaucratic–military dual control traps cooperation in dual dependency:

internally dependent on power networks, externally dependent on capital inflows. Civil society and local enterprises are excluded from decision-making.

3.3 The Mirage of Security Zones: From Protection to Segregated Space

In parts of Asia and Africa, foreign-funded projects are almost always accompanied by security zones—enclaves encircled by walls, checkpoints, and armed guards: a kind of fortified development.

The spatial symbolism is powerful:

- On the map, they demarcate the border between state and foreign capital;
- In society, they mark the distance between people and modernization;
- Psychologically, they draw the boundary between trust and fear.

On the surface, security zones protect expatriates and equipment;
in reality, they symbolize social segregation: development becomes not a shared process but a staged display of power.

This structure directly de-humanizes cooperative relations.
Foreign experts shuttle between dormitories and worksites; local communities are kept outside.
In some countries, project enclaves function as micro-sovereign spaces under separate military–police jurisdiction.

Rolland (2019) observes that such spatial arrangements are widespread along the Belt and Road, embodying the logic of infrastructure as power: those who control roads and ports control the economy and discourse of the state.
Yet this control does not generate social trust.
Field observations show locals often regard these "foreign zones" as another world, while expatriates view "local society" as a latent risk.

In the end, fear drives both sides of the relationship.

3.4 The Elite Economic Closed Loop: Investment, Debt, and Failed Redistribution

Economically, this model produces an elite closed loop.
International funds do not yield broad social benefits; they concentrate in the hands of a few political and business families.
Klitgaard (2013) argues that in low-transparency, weak-accountability settings, external investment readily becomes legitimized rent-seeking.

The operating logic of this closed loop:

1. Governments sign large loans or engineering contracts;
2. The military or oligarchic groups subcontract execution;
3. Profits are absorbed at the top, while debt is socialized;
4. Workers and communities receive only temporary jobs—and inflation.

World Bank (2024) data indicate that in some countries participating in the Belt and Road and regional schemes, infrastructure projects raise aggregate GDP but do not significantly improve employment or livelihoods.
This growth-with-inequality pattern is a hallmark of authoritarian developmentalism.

Basu (2022) contends that such pseudo-growth acts as a social anesthetic: it makes the state appear to be advancing while replicating the old structure.
Local societies are excluded from "modernization"; the power center profits from "cooperation."

3.5 Opinion Architecture: Performative Friendship and a Silenced Public

A further mechanism of authoritarian alliances is opinion monopoly.

Once cooperation is framed as "national honor," dissent is branded "disloyal." Media are tasked with amplifying the brotherhood narrative, not empirical debate.

This propaganda logic serves three functions:
1.   External legitimation: showcasing "unity and stability" to the world;
2.   Internal mobilization: suppressing criticism through nationalist sentiment;
3.   Risk shifting: when projects falter, blaming "external interference."

Diamond (2021) notes that authoritarian states commonly deploy defensive nationalism to manufacture external threats and consolidate internal loyalty. Within this logic, "friendship" itself becomes part of the defense mechanism— not an emotional bond but a political firewall.

Performative friendship is highly theatrical:
embraces and signings on television; segregation and mistrust on the ground.
The public becomes spectator, not participant.

3.6 Institutional Consequences: The Fear Cycle and the Mirage of Modernization

Taken together, the power structure of authoritarian alliances generates a fear–protection–dependency cycle:

Stage I: Fear
- Mechanism: Inflation of internal dissent and external threats
- Appearance: "National security first"
- Substance: Expansion of military and bureaucratic power

Stage II: Protection
- Mechanism: "Special security zones" for foreign capital and personnel

- Appearance: Escorts, segregation, guarded corridors
- Substance: Erosion of civic trust

Stage III: Dependency
- Mechanism: Capital inflows, rising debt, controlled discourse
- Appearance: GDP growth, proclamations of friendship
- Substance: Skewed distribution, absent public legitimacy

This cycle is the true mechanism of the so-called iron friendship.
It looks solid but is brittle;
it appears stable but is fear-ridden;
it resembles development but entrenches dependency.

Slater (2013) calls this the illusion of order: authoritarian regimes maintain surface order through coercion and propaganda while generating structural crisis. This helps explain why many states in the twenty-first century fall into a governance pattern of high security, low trust, and high risk.

Summary

The core of authoritarian alliances is not friendship—it is control.
Through "securitized friendship," the military, bureaucracy, and elites preserve the regime;
through economic and media closures, the power loop reproduces itself;
the people are excluded from decisions, and social trust dissipates.

Hence the fundamental conclusion of this chapter:
the structure of the "iron brotherhood" is not the condensation of trust but the crystallization of fear—
not a symbol of modernization, but the mirror of its failure.

Chapter S4 — The Economic Mirage and Social Dependency: The Politicization of Development and the Silence of Livelihood

4.1 The Illusion of "Development": Statistical Prosperity and Stagnant Lives

In much of the development discourse across Asia and Africa, "growth" is treated as a symbol of regime legitimacy. Governments unveil high-profile infrastructure projects, sign memoranda of understanding, and showcase rising GDP curves to craft a visual spectacle of "national progress."

Yet, as Basu (2022) argues, such growth often amounts to the illusion of diffused development—impressive in statistics, hollow in social structure.

World Bank (2024) data indicate that over the past decade, many state-led investment economies have seen substantial increases in aggregate GDP, while per-capita income, employment, and quality-of-life indicators have stagnated. In other words, "development" becomes a public-relations project rather than a policy for people's livelihoods.

Within this model, economic construction is assigned a political function: it is no longer aimed at relieving poverty but at proving regime effectiveness. Mega-infrastructure becomes a symbol of modernity. Roads, ports, and power plants are used to craft the image of a "strong state," substituting for genuine efforts in institutional reform, universal education, and social protection.

Key features of this engineering legitimacy include:

1. Heavy reliance on external loans and turnkey contracts;
2. Project approvals dominated by the military or bureaucracy;
3. Publicity outpacing real outputs;
4. Short project cycles, limited social returns, and high environmental costs.

This mirage of development forms the economic base of authoritarian alliances—replacing invisible social trust with visible material construction, and masking long-term structural poverty with short-term numbers.

4.2 Debt Politics: The Truth of Cooperation and the Costs of Tomorrow

Rolland (2019) notes that within the Belt and Road and analogous frameworks, "investment" often travels with debt politics—opaque loan terms, short repayment windows, and elevated interest rates. When projects underperform, countries slide into debt dependency.

Such dependency is not only economic but political. Klitgaard (2013) contends that debt is the most discreet instrument of control in authoritarian cooperation: it needs no army yet permanently narrows sovereign decision space.

The mechanisms of debt politics typically include:
- State-guaranteed loans for foreign-funded projects;
- Revenue streams captured by executing firms and upper elites;
- Loss-making projects socialized through the public purse;
- As debt ratios rise, fiscal policy becomes constrained by external stakeholders.

Transparency International (2024) reports that in several participant countries, public debt exceeds 60% of GDP, with more than half of foreign-exchange earnings devoted to servicing infrastructure loans. Many such projects lack viable profit models and serve political symbolism more than economic rationality.

This debt-led development constitutes a modern form of dependency. Evans's (1995) "embedded autonomy" is inverted: the state ceases to be autonomous vis-à-vis external capital and becomes its agent. Development policy is hijacked; budget priorities are set externally; spending on public education, health, and social protection is crowded out.

Here lies the paradox of authoritarian alliances: while waving the banner of "autonomous development," they forfeit autonomy through debt colonialism.

4.3 Employment Structures and the Livelihood Divide: Factories Running, People Watching

Field observation reveals a striking scene: machines roar and towers rise in project zones, yet surrounding communities remain poor.

The root lies in the disconnect between capital inflow and job creation. Foreign projects often operate in closed-loop modes—equipment, inputs, management, and technical staff are imported; local labor is relegated to low-skilled roles.

According to the ILO's *Global Wage Report* (2024), in some countries hosting large infrastructure projects, foreign-funded ventures account for up to 20% of GDP, yet absorb less than 3% of employment.

This pattern prevents growth from translating into social progress. Workers become absent subjects in development narratives—passive spectators to state-centric engineering rather than co-authors of a people-centered future.

Worse, the structure flips social psychology: development generates resentment, not hope. Local residents perceive foreign projects as "belonging to others," while expatriates are seen as symbols of privilege. This is precisely Basu's (2022) trap of civic indifference.

4.4 Elite Redistribution: The Economic Consolidation of Oligarchic Alliances

Economic policy in authoritarian systems is often controlled by a narrow circle of political and business elites. Through state-cooperation projects they gain monopolistic access to resources, forming a transnational oligarchic network.

Typical features include:

1. Government projects outsourced to designated conglomerates;
2. Privatization of public land to political allies;
3. State banks issuing preferential loans to elite ventures;
4. Rents masked in the name of "national interest."

Levitsky and Way (2010) note that competitive authoritarianism does not abolish markets; it domesticates them as tools of power. Economic order seeks compliance over efficiency.

The result is highly concentrated gains, downward mobility for the middle class, and shrinking social mobility. As Kaura (2025) argues in analyzing South Asian political economy:

"Alliances among the military, bureaucracy, and oligarchs transform the national economy into an instrument for stabilizing power, not improving lives."

Under this iron-brotherhood economy, the fruits of development accrue to the few, while the many are left with inflation and unemployment.

4.5 Social Effects: From Hope to Numbness

The greatest harm of the economic mirage is not merely unequal distribution; it is the destruction of the architecture of hope.

When people witness dazzling infrastructure but unchanged lives, when "friendship" is trumpeted but never felt, trust curdles into indifference and expectation into self-mockery.

Diamond (2021) argues that social trust is the bridge between democracy and development. Authoritarian developmentalism demolishes that bridge. The state manufactures a digitalized spectacle of progress, but cannot repair the fissure of trust between state and society.

Accumulated indifference produces a vacuum of legitimacy. In crisis, citizens will not defend the state—because they were never genuinely represented by it.

As Evans (1995) writes:

"A developmental state without social embeddedness is a giant bled dry; it may still walk, but it has no soul."

4.6 From Economic Dependency to Institutional Crisis: Modernity's Aphasia

The economic structure of authoritarian alliances is not genuine modernization but institutional aphasia. Governments endlessly invoke "progress," "cooperation," and "growth," yet cannot speak the words "rights," "equity," or "citizenship."

This absence of language reveals institutional fear:
fear of justice, because it questions rule;
fear of participation, because it unsettles power.

Ultimately, "development" becomes a metaphor for power—a catch-all slogan that conceals social injustice. As Rolland (2019) puts it:

"When development becomes an article of political faith, it loses economic reason."

Long-term consequences include:
- Collapse of public trust;
- Stifled civic innovation;
- Fiscal dependence on debt;
- A widening gap between wealth and political discontent.

Authoritarian alliances appear to be constructing the future while, in fact, reinforcing the past.

Conclusion to Chapter 4: Imbalanced Modernization and a Silenced People

This chapter exposes the central contradiction of authoritarian alliances at the economic level: they pursue legitimacy in the language of "development," yet lose their soul in structures of dependency.

GDP growth cannot conceal social stagnation; capital inflows cannot generate flows of trust. When development is politicized and livelihoods are reduced to statistics, modernization no longer belongs to the people—it becomes a stage for the few.

The authoritarian "economic miracle" is prosperity without a soul:
it builds roads while dismantling trust;
it raises towers while burying hope.

Chapter S5 — The Cultural and Discursive Mirage: The Language of Friendship and the Breakdown of Trust

5.1 Origins of the "Brotherhood Narrative": How Language Constructs Illusion

In the diplomatic lexicon of authoritarian regimes, terms such as "brother," "community of shared destiny," and "all-weather friendship" appear repeatedly. These are not neutral expressions; they are highly politicized emotional devices. This discursive system is not designed to communicate with peoples, but to consolidate a symbolic bond between regimes.

Foucault (1978) argues that discourse is not merely a tool for expressing ideas but a means of producing reality. When a state incessantly repeats "brotherhood," "mutual trust," and "win–win," the words themselves become acts of power—reducing complex political relations to moral narratives and disguising obedience as trust.

Within an authoritarian alliance, "brotherhood" does not signify equality; it signifies subordination. It fashions a paternalistic friendship in which the stronger state plays protector and the weaker state plays the grateful client. This asymmetric relation is packaged as "mutual benefit," but in essence it is structural dependency.

Through constant symbolic repetition in media, diplomatic rhetoric, and propaganda films, the public is made to believe in the authenticity of this "emotional diplomacy." Yet the "language of trust" conceals a simple fact: genuine trust cannot be commanded; it must be practiced.

5.2 The Propaganda Apparatus and the Management of Public Emotion

Media systems in authoritarian states function as factories of legitimacy. Diamond (2021) calls this emotional governance: the regime maintains order by manufacturing external threats and internal unity.

Within this logic, propaganda is not merely informational; it steers emotion and excludes dissent. "Brotherly friendship" is set up as an unquestionable truth. When citizens raise concerns about investment risks or security, they are accused of "damaging the national image" or being "used by external forces."

This opinion-control mechanism operates on three levels:

1. Affective mobilization: translating foreign relations into nationalist sentiment;
2. Cognitive closure: narrowing the bounds of public debate so that people receive only a one-way narrative;
3. Institutional defense: substituting propaganda for transparency and loyalty for accountability.

As a result, public understanding of international cooperation becomes radically simplified—not grounded in economic and social evaluation but in emotion and belief.

Such emotional mobilization yields short-term political gain while corroding social rationality in the long run. As Slater (2013) observes:
"The greatest danger of authoritarianism is not violence but the soothing rhetoric that deprives people of judgment."

5.3 Social Distance: The Performance of Friendship and the Reality Gap

In many cities across Asia and Africa, one finds signage proclaiming "Friendship Road," "Cooperation Square," or "Bridge of Destiny." Yet behind these slogans, expatriates and locals live in two separate worlds.

This spatial segregation of cooperation produces a deep cultural rupture. Foreign engineers shuttle along closed routes between secure zones and hotels; local residents look on from beyond the fence. Psychologically, this separation hardens an othering structure of perception: outsiders are seen as security risks, locals as latent threats.

Hull (2012) notes that the bureaucratic management of social space transforms "governance" into surveillance: people are no longer trusted; they are watched. This is the cultural contradiction of authoritarian cooperation: friendship becomes an exhibition, not a symbiosis.

In interviews, many local youths say they have never spoken with foreign workers nor understood how projects actually operate. What they see are armed patrols and expressways. In such a context, "cooperation" becomes a cold symbol, and "friendship" an imposed slogan.

5.4 Misaligned Identity and Perception: When Faces Become Political Symbols

The author's own field experience attests to this cultural tension. Upon arriving at a certain country's airport, he was subjected to additional screening because his appearance led officials to assume he was Chinese. Once he stated he was a U.S. citizen, the attitude immediately softened.

This difference reveals a latent logic: identity is not a cultural label but a political signal. In authoritarian alliances, appearance, language, and passports are encoded as markers of "friend" or "foe."

Such misrecognition erects psychological barriers at the societal level: people no longer meet as individuals but confront one another as national embodiments. "Where are you from?" becomes a security issue rather than a social one.

Hence, the more frequent the performance of friendship, the deeper the social cleavage. As Basu (2022) notes:
"When development is monopolized by the state, people lose the space to understand one another."

5.5 Religion and Values: The Politicization of Faith and the Absence of Compassion

Many authoritarian states borrow religious language in diplomacy to fortify legitimacy. Slogans such as "shared faith" or "brotherly religion" are used to veil structural inequality. Yet such politicization betrays religion's original ethical spirit.

Foucault (1978) points out that power often invokes morality to package obedience as virtue. When faith is instrumentalized by politics, it loses its dimension of compassion.

Field observation shows two outcomes of this political use of religion:
1.   Domestically: the state enforces social conformity through religious identity, excluding dissent and minorities;
2.   Externally: governments deploy religious affinity as a diplomatic tool, trading "resonance of faith" for political capital.

This religious pragmatism weakens genuine civilizational dialogue. It converts faith from inner cultivation into a component of national image engineering. Thus, even when governments sing hymns of "brotherhood," societies remain bereft of moral trust.

5.6 Media Representation and Ideological Reproduction

Media play a central role in crafting the myth of friendship. Rolland (2019) finds that state-controlled outlets employ visual politics to create the illusion of stability and prosperity: factory smokestacks, smiling workers, handshaking leaders. Off-camera, reality is rife with tension and deprivation.

These images do not record; they normalize perception. By repeatedly displaying scenes of "successful cooperation," the public is inculcated with a trust that requires no doubt. This visual faith becomes a new modality of authoritarian politics: people cease to understand the world rationally and instead believe it passively through images.

Foucault (1978) calls this "knowledge as submission." When propaganda displaces fact, understanding collapses into obedience.

5.7 The Fracture of Trust and the Hollowing of Culture

Trust is the precondition for any civilizational exchange. In authoritarian alliances, trust is reduced to its minimum. Governments trust one another because they share power structures; peoples do not trust one another because they are segregated, misled, and surveilled.

This dual structure hollows out culture. Rituals of cooperation replace genuine exchange; propaganda displaces interpersonal relations; "friendship" becomes political language rather than human sentiment.

As Evans (1995) states: "No state without social embeddedness can generate durable trust." Here, culture ceases to be the soul of society and becomes an ornament of rule. True civilizational trust can be born only from civil society, not from the stagecraft of authoritarian diplomacy.

Summary: When Language Loses Sincerity, Friendship Loses Warmth

The authoritarian alliance's false warmth at the level of culture and public discourse shows a stark paradox: governments manufacture unity through "brotherly language," even as propaganda and segregation dissolve genuine bonds among people.

Language becomes ritualized; trust is politicized. The propaganda machine supplants dialogue, and visual mirage supplants reality.

Such "friendship" is symbolic domination: it makes people chant the same slogans while drifting further apart.
Thus, when a country must rely on slogans and guards to prove friendship, that is not the success of cooperation—it is the absence of trust.

Chapter S6 — From Fear to Hope: A Night When Military Power Replaced Law

6.1 Aziz Bhatti Road: Absurdity and Shock on a City Boulevard

In October 2025 in Lahore, Pakistan, I witnessed a scene that laid bare the truth of an entire system.

Around 1 a.m., I took a taxi to the airport for a 4 a.m. international flight. The streets were quiet, the city asleep. Our car moved along Aziz Bhatti Road — a broad urban artery linking residential areas to the airport, a normal public route.

As we approached an intersection, armed soldiers raised their hands to stop us. The driver slowed and pulled over. One soldier approached and demanded, in a commanding tone, to see identification.
I immediately took out my U.S. passport, opened it to the photo page, and held it up: "I'm an American citizen, going to the airport."

He glanced briefly and walked away without a word. Moments later, a higher-ranking officer stepped forward, his voice harsher, again demanding the passport. I showed it without handing it over. "I will not surrender it," I said clearly.

He gave no reply. Instead, he reached out suddenly and snatched the passport from my hand.
The air froze — no explanation, no reason, only the certainty of force.

"You cannot take my passport! This is illegal!" I protested.
He ignored me and ordered the driver: "Turn back. Take another road."

The driver, visibly afraid, whispered: "Sir, this area is controlled by the army. Foreigners cannot pass through. We must go around."

144

We made a U-turn into narrow side streets and waited at another checkpoint. After about fifteen minutes, the passport was returned — not to me, but to the driver, who handed it back quietly. "It's okay now," he murmured.

There was no explanation, no record, no apology. This was not a security procedure but a performance of power — a declaration that the soldiers, not the law, rule the city.

6.2 The Theater of Privilege: When "Security" Becomes a Display of Arrogance

That incident on Aziz Bhatti Road was no isolated case; it was a symbol of authoritarian culture.
Under the name of "security," the military creates forbidden zones and demonstrates privilege in public space.
Efficiency and legality do not matter — only that people fear them.

As Foucault (1978) wrote in *Discipline and Punish*:

"Power does not need violence to prove itself; it only needs violence to appear natural."

At that moment on the road, both security and dignity died.
It was not merely an insult to a foreigner but a profanation of the nation's own rule of law.

6.3 The Instinct of Institutions: From Colonial Legacy to Military Dominance

Such behavior was not accidental.
As Alavi (1972) analyzed, many post-colonial armies inherited the colonial logic of rule: they appear to defend the state while actually controlling it.

In Pakistan, the military has long stood above civil government and the judiciary, becoming the true center of power.
Kaura (2025) notes: "Behind every civilian administration lurks the shadow of the army."

Thus the officer's arrogance was not personal rudeness but institutional reflex — a system that teaches soldiers to believe they embody the state, and that the state exists for them.

6.4 The Psychology of Fear

Later the driver told me: "Sir, locals are afraid too. They never argue with soldiers."

That sentence revealed everything. The army could treat foreigners this way because it has long treated its own people the same.
In such a structure, fear is institutionalized and silence normalized.

As Hull (2012) observes:

"When power rests on fear, obedience is rebranded as patriotism."

Fear becomes the common language of society.
People seek safety within fear and forget freedom.

6.5 Diplomatic Action: The Last Frontier of Civilization

At the airport, I immediately contacted both governments.

I reported the incident to the U.S. Embassy in Pakistan, requesting investigation and protection;
and I submitted a formal protest letter to the Pakistani ambassador in Washington, demanding an apology from the military.

"Such behavior is deeply shocking and entirely unacceptable in any civilized country.
The officer's conduct violated basic international protocol and betrayed Pakistan's own national dignity."

The letters were not merely acts of self-protection but appeals to civilization itself. They reminded the world that true friendship among nations rests on respect and the rule of law.

6.6 The Cycle of Power and Poverty

Incidents like this lie at the root of Pakistan's poverty and stagnation.
When resources are spent on the military and "stability" rather than education and healthcare,
both social trust and economic growth are drained away.

According to the International Labour Organization (2024),
countries with heavy military interference show per-capita GDP growth rates more than 40 percent lower than democracies.
The barrel of the gun is not aimed at the enemy — it is aimed at the future of development.

6.7 From Fear to Hope: The Beginning of Awakening

Yet fear is not the end.
After humiliation and anger, awakening often begins with the defense of personal dignity.

Diamond (2021) writes:

"Democracy begins not with institutions but with the moment anger is made rational."

A new generation — students, journalists, teachers, and citizen groups — is learning to rebuild trust and public space through non-violent means.
They are learning to speak the truth — even when the price is silencing — and they are no longer silent.

6.8 Epilogue: The End of Fear Is the Beginning of Hope

That night proved one thing: fear is not a psychological accident; it is an engineered system.
But hope is also an engineering project — it begins the moment an individual refuses to be humiliated.

When a nation learns to respect the passport of every stranger, it has finally begun to respect its own people.

From fear to hope,
from privilege to rule of law,
from gun power to human rights —
that is the only path to the rebirth of civilization.

Chapter S7 — Rebuilding Institutions: Truth, Trust and Law as the Roots of the Nation

7.1 After Fear: The Silence that Extends from Person to System

When soldiers on Lahore's Aziz Bhatti Road seized my passport, I was not the only victim.

That moment of helplessness — the forced U-turn, the waiting, the quiet return of a document — was a miniature of how millions of Pakistanis interact with authority every day.

When power lacks restraint, fear becomes the default language.
People learn to avoid conflict rather than solve it;
to please power rather than oversee it.
This habitual silence corrodes the soul of a nation.

7.2 Truth: The First Medicine for a Diseased System

Every reconstruction must begin with truth.

Truth is not only the statement of facts but the starting point of responsibility.
A nation without truth can sustain stability only through lies;
faith without truth eventually becomes an instrument of fear.

To rebuild truth:

1.   Create independent investigative mechanisms — the military and government alike must be subject to civilian oversight.

2.   Protect whistleblowers — freedom of the press is the immune system of institutions.

3.   Publish data and procedures — make power transparent, not mystical.

As Klitgaard (2013) put it:

"Sunlight is the best disinfectant — but only if the window can open."

7.3 Trust: The Rebirth of the Social Contract

Fear destroys trust; rebuilding it means redistributing power.

(1) Trust grows from equality.
When uniforms stand above the law, trust cannot exist.
All public servants, including the military, must be equally bound by the constitution.

(2) Trust grows from participation.
Citizens must be part of decision-making — not objects of rule but partners in governance.

(3) Trust grows from education.
Education should not produce obedience but critical thinking and empathy.
A teacher who encourages students to question does more for democracy than a thousand political speeches.

7.4 Rule of Law: Setting Boundaries for Power

The rule of law is not a sentence written in a constitution;
it is a mechanism of national self-restraint.

To achieve it, Pakistan must enact three foundational reforms:
1. Judicial independence — appointments and budgets detached from the executive.

2.   Civilian oversight of police and military — establish public accountability bodies.

3.   Civic constitutional education — teaching that rights and duties are inseparable.

As Basu (2022) writes:

"Development is not about building more roads, but building bridges of justice."

7.5 Institutional Redesign: From Centralization to Local Autonomy

For decades, power has concentrated in capitals while local governments became mere executors.
Modernization must shift toward decentralization and fiscal autonomy.
*   Local councils should be directly elected.
*   Budgets and taxes must be transparent.
*   Social programs should be community-driven, not military-administered.

When resources return to the people, politics ceases to be a game of privilege.

7.6 Moral Modernization: The Inner Repair of Civilization

Rebuilding institutions is not just technical; it is moral renewal.
A truly modern state is not bound by fear but rooted in empathy.

Three paths of moral modernization:
1.   Faith to conscience — religion must defend justice, not cover power.
2.   Economy to fairness — wealth must serve society, not entrench privilege.

3.   Politics to responsibility — legitimacy comes from the courage to be accountable.

When faith and reason reunite, a nation's soul awakens from fear.

7.7 International Insight: From "Iron Brotherhood" to "Institutional Friendship"

The so-called "iron brotherhood," built on mutual military protection, inevitably rusts.
Sustainable cooperation must become institutional friendship:
- Bridges of law instead of security pacts;
- Civic exchanges instead of military drills;
- Trust and consensus instead of deterrence and control.

Only when relations rise above uniforms and slogans can nations move toward genuine modern civilization.

7.8 The Roots of Civilization Must Grow in the People

Rebuilding institutions is not fixing machinery but rewriting a nation's soul.
Truth is the root, trust the water, law the light.
Together they nurture a new country —
one where citizens no longer fear soldiers,
passports no longer symbolize threat,
but become extensions of dignity.

"Fear ends where faith begins — and faith is fulfilled when law protects the weak."
— *ButterflyMan*

7.9 The Mirage of Sino-Pakistani Friendship: Deformed Alliances and the Return to Humanity

For decades, the relationship between China and Pakistan has been hailed as an
iron brotherhood —
a "community of shared destiny," a "partnership for all seasons," a model of
South-South cooperation beyond ideology.

But anyone who walks through Lahore's streets and factories at night,
seeing soldiers seize foreign passports,
citizens silenced by fear,
and workers still struggling in poverty,
understands that this "iron" is not warm trust — it is a cold shackle.

1 Deformed Political and Economic Structures

What is described as cooperation has become a symbiotic authoritarian structure.
On the surface: trade and investment.
In reality: two authoritarian systems in mutual dependence —
one providing capital and technology, the other political obedience and strategic
depth.

Benefits concentrate in elite and military circles.
Entrepreneurs, workers, and youth — the real vitality of the economy — are
excluded.

It is a monstrous hybrid of economic and political dependence,
sustained not by popular will but by fear, control, and propaganda.

As Kaura (2025) observes:

"When development is defined as the ability to control others,

cooperation ceases to be win-win and becomes shared servitude.”

2 An Unsustainable Illusion

An alliance built on mutual dictatorship is not friendship but the warmth of shared fear.

Chinese state capitalism and Pakistan's military regime mirror each other:
- Both suppress civil society in the name of "stability."
- Both hide corruption and monopoly behind "national security."
- Both replace personal dignity with nationalist pride.

Such cooperation cannot last.

It lacks public consent and moral legitimacy.

When expression, oversight, and choice are denied,

economic prosperity becomes a spectacle sustained by fear.

Any prosperity built on oppression ultimately self-destructs.

3 A Warning to Chinese Citizens: The Price of Brotherhood

Today, Chinese nationals in Pakistan require *special protection* — armed guards, passes, escorts.

The irony is stark:

if brothers need guns to visit one another, is it still friendship?

Entrepreneurs and engineers, told they are walking the "road of cooperation,"

are in fact traveling a path that can be swallowed by fear at any moment.

They enter a system controlled by the military,

where power trades for money and silence buys safety.

This is not development but collusion;

154

not friendship but mutual hostage-taking.

4 A Warning to the Chinese Government: History Will Not Tolerate Deformed Alliances

Beijing must understand:
supporting dictatorships, trading loyalty for arms, or buying obedience with investment
creates only temporary dependence — never respect.

Every regime that refused reform in the name of "security," "unity," or "prosperity"
has ended in isolation, collapse, and internal revolt.

People do not fear forever.
They may be silent for ten or twenty years,
but sooner or later, fear yields to dignity,
and conscience disarms the gun.

5 The Return to Humanity: The Only Way Forward

The future of both China and Pakistan
lies not in weapons, ports, or projects,
but in their shared rediscovery of humanity and human rights.

Only when both nations admit that
- people matter more than states,
- freedom is dearer than stability, and
- rights are truer than slogans,

can cooperation evolve from control to coexistence, from interest to trust.
The only safe path for any autocrat

is not to cling to power but to relinquish it.
Only when rulers become ordinary citizens
do they finally approach freedom.

Epilogue — True Brotherhood Cannot Be Built on Fear

If China and Pakistan are ever to have a genuine future together,
friendship must return to the people,
economy to its creators,
and trust to law and respect.

Only humanity can heal deformity;
only freedom can end fear.

"No empire built on fear has ever survived compassion."
— *ButterflyMan*

Appendix 3:

From Suharto to Reformasi—and Beyond: Lessons for Pakistan from Indonesia's Democratic Transition

From Suharto to Reformasi—and Beyond: Lessons for Pakistan from Indonesia's Democratic Transition

A Comparative Study of Political Economy, Society, and Civil–Military Balance

ButterflyMan
Independent researcher, author, entrepreneur

Abstract

Indonesia and Pakistan, both populous Muslim-majority nations with post-colonial histories and long experiences of military or authoritarian dominance, diverged sharply after 1998. Indonesia's transition from the Suharto "New Order" to the Reformasi era of decentralised democracy has produced tangible economic and social gains. Pakistan, meanwhile, remains constrained by recurrent military interventions and fragile civilian institutions. This article presents a comparative analysis of their political economies, cultural structures, and governance systems. It argues that Indonesia's model—crisis-triggered reform, institutional decentralisation, and gradual civil–military rebalancing—offers critical lessons for Pakistan's democratic and developmental future.

Introduction

Indonesia and Pakistan share structural features: both are majority-Muslim, possess large populations exceeding 240 million, and occupy pivotal regional positions. Each inherited colonial administrative legacies and experienced periods of military or authoritarian rule. Yet their trajectories over the past quarter-century diverged dramatically. Indonesia's transition from the Suharto "New Order" (1966–1998) to a decentralised democracy is widely regarded as a case study in reform following crisis; Pakistan, conversely, continues to wrestle with cycles of civilian–military imbalance and economic fragility. This chapter evaluates economic size, governance, social development, and institutional structures in both states to ask: Can Pakistan follow Indonesia's path—and if so, when and how?

1. Country Profiles and Key Macroeconomic Indicators

1.1 Indonesia

World Bank data show Indonesia's economy approaching the US$1.5 trillion threshold, with GDP (current US$) in the trillions and a steady upward trend since the early 2000s; GDP per capita (current US$) now hovers in the mid-$4,000s. Multiple sources put 2024 nominal GDP near US$1.4 trillion and per-capita income around US$4,900–4,950. Post-Suharto, Indonesia consolidated its position as Southeast Asia's largest economy and an upper-middle-income country. Poverty reduction has been substantial, with per-capita income more than tripling since the late 1990s, and reform narratives highlight decentralisation, competitive elections, and a growing internal market.

1.2 Pakistan

Pakistan's nominal GDP is substantially smaller. World Bank series place GDP (current US$) in the low hundreds of billions and per-capita income around US$1,500–1,600. Although Pakistan's PPP size is larger, macro-volatility, external financing dependence, and security shocks have repeatedly interrupted growth. These indicators position Pakistan in the lower-middle-income tier, with significant structural constraints in industrial depth and fiscal capacity.

1.3 Comparative Snapshot

Indonesia's economy is roughly three to four times Pakistan's in nominal terms; per-capita output is about three times higher. Social metrics also diverge: adult literacy approximates 96% in Indonesia (2020) versus the high-50s in Pakistan

(2019 estimates), and health-infrastructure proxies such as hospital beds per 1,000 inhabitants favour Indonesia. These gaps underscore how institutional and policy choices produced different development paths despite demographic similarities.

2. Methodological Note

This study adopts a comparative-historical approach combining macroeconomic indicators (GDP, GDP per capita), human-development proxies (literacy, health infrastructure), and institutional milestones (constitutional change, decentralisation statutes). Data sources include the World Bank World Development Indicators (WDI), encyclopedic summaries for historical chronology, major media and policy analyses on recent legal changes in Indonesia, and specialised think-tank pieces on Pakistan's civil–military balance. The article privileges primary statistical sources for quantitative claims and triangulates interpretive claims with multiple reputable analyses.

3. Historical and Political Trajectories

3.1 Indonesia under Suharto and the Reformasi Era

Suharto's "New Order" regime (1966–1998) concentrated power within a centralised presidency and an expansive military apparatus (Angkatan Bersenjata Republik Indonesia, ABRI). The dwifungsi or "dual function" doctrine legitimised military involvement in both national defence and internal political administration. The 1997–1998 Asian Financial Crisis precipitated regime collapse; the rupiah's sharp depreciation, inflation, and social unrest led to Suharto's resignation on 21 May 1998. His departure inaugurated the Reformasi period: competitive elections in 1999, a sweeping "big-bang" decentralisation in 2001 that devolved resources and authority to districts, and an iterative strengthening of civil liberties and party competition. While corruption and rent-seeking persisted, the political system moved from concentrated authoritarianism toward a more pluralistic equilibrium.

3.2 Pakistan's Political Dynamics and Military Dominance

Pakistan's post-independence history is punctuated by coups (1958, 1977, 1999) and recurrent extra-constitutional interventions. The armed forces have built a dense institutional presence across the state and economy, often described as "military capital" or "Milbus." Cycles of weak party governance, intra-elite competition, and persistent external threats have sustained the military's role as the pre-eminent arbiter. Regular elections take place, but civilian governments typically operate under constraints imposed by the security establishment and intelligence services. Analyses in 2025 reaffirm that Pakistan's core governance challenge remains an enduring civil–military imbalance.

4. Why Authoritarian or Military Rule Persists—and How Indonesia Broke the Model

4.1 Persistence: The "Guardian of the Nation" Narrative

In both countries, militaries framed themselves as guardians of national unity amid perceived internal and external threats—legitimising exceptional roles in politics. In Indonesia's New Order, developmental authoritarianism delivered order, macro-stability, and visible infrastructure, offsetting the regime's coercion in the public mind. In Pakistan, decades of security dilemmas (India, Afghanistan, militancy) and repeated governance failures deepened reliance on the military as the guarantor of stability. Weak decentralisation and accountability structures prolonged this pattern.

4.2 Indonesia's Breakthrough: Crisis, Coalition Shift, and Institutional Redesign

Indonesia's transition was triggered by legitimacy collapse during the Asian Financial Crisis and catalysed by student protest, elite defections, and international scrutiny. Critical reforms followed: fiscal and administrative devolution to districts, direct local elections, and the rollback of the military's formal political role. This did not eliminate military influence, but it re-anchored Indonesia's political economy in competitive civilian institutions and multi-level accountability. The Reformasi "big-bang" decentralisation is widely cited as a distinctive, path-altering innovation.

5. Social, Cultural, and Institutional Dimensions

Indonesia's archipelagic diversity—over 17,000 islands and hundreds of languages—compelled institutional responses that bring government closer to citizens. Decentralisation served both to relieve centre–periphery tensions and to create new arenas for accountability. Pakistan's analogous diversity (Punjabi, Sindhi, Baloch, Pashtun, and others) has typically been managed through centralised control, producing periodic provincial resentments and legitimacy deficits.

Culturally, Indonesia's Pancasila ideology attempts to balance religion, nationalism, and pluralism; by contrast, Pakistan's Islamisation drive under Zia-ul-Haq re-weighted the political field toward religious identity and institutions, with mixed consequences for pluralism. Social indicators highlight divergence: adult literacy around 96% for Indonesia (2020) versus under 60% for Pakistan (2019), infant mortality far lower in Indonesia, and substantially higher hospital-bed density in Indonesia. These social investments underpin democratic legitimacy by improving everyday state capacity and citizen trust.

6. Economic Structure, Performance, and Outlook

6.1 Indonesia

Indonesia's economy has diversified from hydrocarbons toward manufacturing and services, as reflected in the long-run decline of oil rents as a share of GDP and robust consumer-led growth. Annual real growth has averaged around 5%, punctuated by shocks (1998 crisis; 2008–09 global crisis; COVID-19). The "Golden Indonesia 2045" agenda articulates a mid-century vision with targets for per-capita income near US$25,000, predicated on human-capital upgrades and domestic processing of critical minerals. Governance risks persist—corruption, uneven provincial development, and, in 2025, controversy around a military-law revision expanding the scope for officers to occupy civilian posts—but baseline institutions remain more competitive and transparent than during the New Order.

6.2 Pakistan

Pakistan's growth has been prone to stop-go dynamics, shaped by balance-of-payments pressures, fiscal constraints, energy shortages, and political shocks. Recent growth readings underscore modest recovery but from a low base. Structural issues—narrow tax base, low export complexity, weak regulatory credibility, and the crowding-out effects of the security sector's economic footprint—continue to weigh on investment and productivity. A durable growth pivot requires macro-stabilisation paired with institutional reforms that reduce uncertainty and improve the returns to private enterprise.

6.3 Comparative Outlook

Indonesia's wider domestic market, stronger average human-capital indicators, and post-1998 institutional reforms explain its superior performance. Pakistan's demographic potential could yield a dividend if matched by decentralisation, education reform, and credible civilian governance. Over a generation, sustained reform could narrow gaps in income, health, and institutional quality.

7. Governance, Democracy, and Institutional Reform

Indonesia demonstrates incremental but tangible democratic consolidation: repeated competitive elections, a freer press, and multi-level governance anchored in districts and provinces. Democratic quality has varied—analysts warn of periodic backsliding risks and of 2025's military-law change—but the overall direction since 1999 remains more pluralist than during the Suharto era.

Pakistan's parliamentary framework coexists with entrenched military influence. Local government remains underpowered, and institutional capture hinders rule-of-law consolidation. Comparative work argues that Pakistan can adapt Indonesia's approach to reducing military interventionism through phased constitutional reform, professionalised civilian security oversight, and empowered provincial systems. The 2025 debate on Pakistan's civil–military balance, including senior-rank promotions and public-order roles, highlights the urgency of structural fixes.

8. Sectoral Deep-Dive Comparisons

8.1 Education and Literacy

Indonesia's adult-literacy rate—approximately 96%—reflects decades of primary-education expansion and improved access; Pakistan's adult-literacy remains below 60% on recent UNESCO/World Bank series, with gender and regional disparities. Expanding female education and vocational pathways is central to labour-productivity gains.

8.2 Health Systems

Hospital-bed density is a coarse but illustrative proxy of system capacity: Indonesia's rate exceeds Pakistan's, consistent with better outcomes in infant and maternal mortality. Pakistan's fiscal constraints and uneven provincial delivery contribute to access gaps; Indonesia's decentralised system has its own inefficiencies but offers citizen-level accountability mechanisms.

8.3 Fiscal and Intergovernmental Architecture

Indonesia's "big-bang" decentralisation transferred expenditure responsibilities and revenue-sharing to districts quickly, followed by iterative legal refinements to manage capacity and corruption risks. Pakistan's 18th Amendment devolved competencies to provinces, but implementation gaps and administrative overlap continue to limit effectiveness. A district-centred fiscal federalism—clear assignment of functions, formula-based transfers, and local revenue authority—could replicate more of Indonesia's accountability dynamics.

8.4 Security and Civilian Oversight

Indonesia removed the military's reserved parliamentary seats and narrowed formal political roles, even if informal influence remains. In 2025, a new law permitting more officer placements in civilian bodies sparked protests, signalling active societal vigilance. Pakistan's path requires statutory constraints on the military's political entrepreneurship and transparent oversight of defence-linked economic enterprises, drawing on scholarship about "Milbus."

9. Scenarios for Pakistan: From "Praetorian Trap" to Democratic Dividend

Scenario A: Incremental Drift (Status Quo).
Modest macro-stabilisation without structural reform keeps growth low, fiscal space tight, and public frustration high. Civilian governments rotate without

consolidating authority; military influence remains decisive. Human-capital gaps persist.

Scenario B: Shock-Triggered Opening (Crisis Window).

A severe economic or political shock fractures elite consensus. A reform coalition negotiates a limited pact: credible elections, time-bound civil–military rebalancing, and a decentralisation package that empowers districts within a clearer fiscal framework. International partners condition support on measurable institutional milestones.

Scenario C: Reform-Led Transition (Planned).

Political leadership launches a "Prosperous Pakistan 2047" agenda echoing Indonesia 2045: targets for literacy, health, export complexity, and subnational service delivery; a civil-service modernisation and judicial-reform track; and staged, monitorable steps to professionalise civil–military boundaries. This scenario maximises legitimacy and investment by signalling commitment and predictability.

10. Policy Roadmap for Pakistan (Adaptive to Local Realities)

1.   Constitutional Sequencing for Civil–Military Balance.

•   Codify a clear separation of military command from civilian policy-making, with statutory bans on active-duty officers holding civilian posts (except under tightly defined emergencies approved by parliament and courts).

•   Establish an independent Defence Accounts and Assets Commission to audit military-owned enterprises, publish accounts, and propose divestitures to a sovereign holding fund.

2.   District-Centred Decentralisation.

•   Move from province-heavy devolution to function-specific district assignments (primary health, K-8 schooling, local roads and water), financed by formula-based transfers and limited local taxation powers.

• Create a District Performance Compact framework with output-based grants and citizen scorecards, echoing Indonesia's iterative "big-bang" refinements.

3.   Human-Capital Sprint (Girls' Education + Primary Health).

• Target universal lower-secondary completion within 10 years; deploy conditional cash transfers tied to girls' attendance.

• Expand primary-care networks with standardised packages and digital monitoring; ring-fence allocations equal to a minimum share of GDP for health and education until literacy surpasses 85%.

4.   Export Complexity and Industrial Deepening.

• Prioritise sectors where Pakistan can rapidly climb value chains (textiles-to-technical textiles, agriprocessing, light engineering).

• Implement predictable tariffs, duty-drawbacks, and technology-adoption credits; publish five-year schedules to reduce policy uncertainty.

5.   Rule-of-Law and Administrative Justice.

• Establish time-bound commercial courts with e-filing and strict case-management; digitise land and collateral registries to expand SME credit.

• Protect an independent media and freedom-of-information statutes to strengthen accountability.

6.   Crisis-Preparedness Playbook.

• Pre-negotiate IMF and bilateral contingencies with structural-reform tranches; create a cross-party fiscal council to depoliticise stabilisation choices.

• Maintain a social-protection shock-absorber (targeted cash transfers) to protect the poorest during adjustment.

7.   National Vision and Monitoring.

• Launch Prosperous Pakistan 2047, aligning milestones with SDGs: literacy 90%, infant mortality <20/1,000, hospital beds ≥1.0/1,000, export/GDP ≥20%.

• Publish an annual Civil–Military Balance Scorecard tracking legal compliance, budget transparency, and civilian oversight indicators.

11. Timing: When Might a "Reformasi-Style" Shift Occur?

Indonesia's 1998 transition offers a caution and a clue: crisis alone is insufficient without prepared reformers and credible institutional pathways. Pakistan's window could open via a fiscal-balance crisis, political stalemate, or external shock—but durable change will require (a) a reform coalition willing to negotiate red lines with the security establishment, (b) a decentralisation blueprint that channels citizen pressure downward into service delivery, and (c) quick, visible wins in schools, clinics, and local infrastructure to validate democracy. A pragmatic horizon is a decade if reforms start now.

12. Risks and Mitigations

- Risk of Backsliding (Indonesia's 2025 Law as Warning).

Expanded military privileges can creep back into politics, undermining gains. Mitigation: embed bright-line legal prohibitions, independent constitutional courts, and civil-society watchdogs.

- Local Capture under Decentralisation.

District elites may entrench patronage. Mitigation: performance-based grants, transparent procurement, citizen feedback loops, and rotation policies for administrators.

- Fiscal Space Constraints.

Social-sector scaling requires money. Mitigation: broaden the tax base (documented property, digital payments), reduce untargeted subsidies, and sequence reform to protect the poorest.

- Security Shocks.

External or internal security events could derail reform. Mitigation: institutionalise civilian-led national-security councils and contingency budgeting.

13. Conclusion

Indonesia's journey from Suharto's authoritarianism to a competitive, decentralised democracy demonstrates that transformation in large Muslim-majority societies is achievable when crisis catalyses reform, power is distributed, and institutions mature. Pakistan—though burdened by structural inequities and military dominance—possesses comparable potential. The core lesson is clear: economic credibility, institutional reform, and civilian accountability can convert public faith into broad-based progress. The Indonesian precedent does not just mirror possibilities for Pakistan; it maps a route—from fear to reform, from power to people.

References

Associated Press. (2023, August 16). Indonesia's leader says it can join leading economies by 2045 if it continues educational reforms.

Blog of the International Association of Constitutional Law (IACL-AIDC). (2025, April 29). Indonesia's new military law and the ghost of consensus-based constitutional transition.

Britannica. (2024). Indonesia after Suharto.

Council on Foreign Relations. (2020). The revival of military rule in Asia. (Context on "guardian of the nation" framing).

CountryEconomy. (2024). Indonesia and Pakistan economic indicators. (Comparative GDP snapshots).

Middle East Institute (Kaura, V.). (2025, May 30). Deepening Pakistan's enduring civil–military imbalance.

Princeton: Innovations for Successful Societies. (n.d.). Decentralizing authority after Suharto: Indonesia's "big-bang," 1998–2010.

Reuters. (2025, March 19). Indonesia's rights groups urge parliament not to pass military law.

UNESCO/World Bank. (2020–2024). Literacy rate, adult total (% of people ages 15 and above). Indonesia and Pakistan series.

World Bank. (2024). GDP (current US$): Indonesia; Pakistan.

World Bank. (2024). GDP per capita (current US$): Indonesia.

World Bank. (2024). Hospital beds (per 1,000 people): Indonesia; Pakistan.

AP News. (2025, March 20). Why Indonesia's new military law is alarming pro-democracy activists and rights groups.

Appendix 4:

THE RIGHT TO REFUSE

THE RIGHT TO REFUSE

The Right to Refuse: Constitutionalizing Lawful Disobedience and Self-Defense in Military Ethics — Lessons from Indonesia, Pakistan, and Beyond

ButterflyMan
Independent Researcher, Author, and Entrepreneur

Abstract

Military obedience has long been regarded as the cornerstone of discipline and state security. Yet history demonstrates that blind obedience, untempered by conscience or law, can transform an army from a national protector into an instrument of internal oppression. From Latin America's military juntas to the Middle East's praetorian regimes, and from Southeast Asia to Africa, soldiers have repeatedly been ordered to suppress their own people in the name of stability. This article advances a new global doctrine: the Right and Duty of Lawful Refusal, whereby soldiers are constitutionally empowered to reject, resist, or act in self-defense against manifestly unlawful domestic orders. Drawing upon comparative case studies from Indonesia, Pakistan, Myanmar, Cambodia, Egypt, Nigeria, Chile, and Brazil, the paper situates this principle within democratic theory, international humanitarian law, and military professionalism. It proposes a model constitutional clause — integrating lawful refusal, self-defense, and commander accountability — as a universal safeguard against authoritarian relapse. The argument reframes military professionalism as fidelity to constitutional law rather than to rulers, thereby uniting discipline with moral courage. The study concludes that institutionalizing this principle is essential for any modern democracy seeking to reconcile security with human dignity.

Keywords: Civil–Military Relations, Constitutional Reform, Lawful Refusal, Military Ethics, Democratic Transition, Global South

Introduction

Throughout modern history, the military has been both the guardian and the gravedigger of democracy. The same institution entrusted with national defense has, in many states, turned its weapons inward—against the citizens it swore to protect. This contradiction lies at the heart of political development across much of the Global South, where armies emerged as the most organized organs of postcolonial power. From Indonesia under Suharto to Pakistan under Zia and Musharraf, from Egypt's Supreme Council to Nigeria's barracks governments, the uniform became the visible face of the state. The soldier's creed of obedience—once designed to protect the republic—was gradually transformed into a justification for subjugating it.

The problem is not military strength itself, but the absence of lawful boundaries defining when obedience becomes complicity. Traditional military education often frames obedience as absolute, assuming that hierarchy ensures order. Yet history reveals that unquestioning obedience enables atrocities: from Latin America's "dirty wars" to massacres in Southeast Asia and Africa. Soldiers who might have acted with conscience were instead conditioned to equate disobedience with treason. Consequently, obedience became detached from legality, and loyalty to command eclipsed loyalty to law.

This paper seeks to reverse that moral hierarchy. It argues that in every professional military force, obedience must be subordinate to legality and guided by conscience, anchored in constitutional supremacy. The right and duty of soldiers to refuse unlawful orders is not an act of mutiny; it is the ethical defense of the state itself. When a soldier refuses to kill unarmed civilians, detain political opponents, or silence the press, he or she is not betraying command but preserving the republic's moral core.

Historical context and moral evolution

The 20th century's most profound shift in military ethics began at Nuremberg, where "I was following orders" ceased to be a defense for crimes against humanity. The trials established a universal principle: individual responsibility surpasses superior command. This principle later shaped

Germany's *Soldiers' Law* (1956), Israel's "Kafr Qassem" precedent (1957), and South Africa's post-apartheid constitution (1996). Each case transformed the soldier's duty from passive obedience to active legality. Yet, despite this evolution, most constitutions in Asia, Africa, and the Muslim world have never codified this standard. Their military codes continue to demand unconditional obedience, allowing regimes to weaponize patriotism against their own people.

In Indonesia, the 1998 *Reformasi* movement dismantled Suharto's *dwifungsi* doctrine, which had embedded the army in political administration. Yet the 2025 re-amendment allowing active officers to hold civil posts shows the fragility of democratic gains. In Pakistan, repeated coups entrenched what Ayesha Siddiqa (2007) termed *Milbus*—a military capitalism that blurs the line between defense and governance. In Egypt, the military's self-proclaimed guardianship of the nation has produced a permanent state of emergency. Nigeria oscillates between barracks rule and fragile democracy, its soldiers often deployed domestically in the name of security. Across these examples, the unifying thread is not religion or culture but the absence of a constitutional mechanism empowering soldiers to say "No."

Research problem and scope

The central question of this study is therefore both ethical and institutional: How can modern states reconcile the need for military discipline with the imperative of moral and legal responsibility? This question is not confined to any one region. It extends from the Islamic republics of South Asia to the secular militaries of Latin America and Africa, wherever power has become insulated from accountability. The comparative scope of this article thus includes Indonesia and Pakistan as core cases, while drawing auxiliary evidence from Myanmar, Cambodia, Egypt, Nigeria, Chile, and Brazil. These nations together represent the spectrum of authoritarian entrenchment and democratic recovery.

Through cross-regional analysis, the study identifies three recurring patterns in the evolution of military rule:

1. The Guardian Myth: the army as "protector of national unity," used to justify intervention.

2.	The Developmental Bargain: exchange of political control for economic growth or order.

3.	The Constitutional Vacuum: absence of clauses clarifying limits of internal deployment and legality of refusal.

This paper's thesis is that enduring democratization requires not merely civilian oversight of the military but constitutional empowerment of the military's conscience. Soldiers must be trained, legally protected, and morally obliged to disobey orders that violate constitutional rights or target domestic populations. Moreover, when superiors enforce unlawful commands through coercion, subordinates must possess the right of proportionate self-defense and the temporary authority to restrain or detain their commanders until civilian law intervenes.

Contribution and significance

By synthesizing lessons from post-authoritarian transitions across the Global South, this study contributes to three overlapping fields:

1.	Comparative constitutional law, by proposing a model clause— *Article X: Civilian Supremacy and Lawful Refusal of Unlawful Orders*— that can be adapted across jurisdictions.

2.	Civil–military relations, by reframing professionalism as loyalty to law rather than to hierarchy.

3.	Human rights and international ethics, by embedding the Nuremberg principle and the right of self-defense within national legal systems.

This approach challenges the false dichotomy between obedience and chaos. True discipline arises not from blind submission but from moral clarity within lawful boundaries. Armies governed by conscience do not weaken the state; they strengthen its legitimacy. Citizens who trust their soldiers are less likely to fear their government, and nations built on trust are less likely to collapse into authoritarianism.

Structure of the article

The remainder of this paper proceeds as follows. Section 2 reviews the global scholarship on military obedience, constitutionalism, and the ethical transformation of command responsibility. Section 3 presents eight comparative cases illustrating diverse trajectories of civil–military evolution. Section 4 formulates the theoretical framework—"Obedience to Law above Command"—grounded in international law and moral philosophy. Section 5 introduces the proposed constitutional model, integrating lawful refusal and self-defense clauses. Section 6 outlines institutional safeguards against mutiny, ensuring that lawful disobedience strengthens rather than destabilizes military hierarchy. Section 7 discusses comparative findings and reform lessons for transitional states. Section 8 concludes with policy implications and a call for a universal *Code of Ethical Command* applicable across all militaries.

In an age where technology multiplies the power of violence, the moral compass of those who wield it becomes civilization's final defense. The right to refuse unlawful orders is therefore not merely a legal reform; it is humanity's safeguard against itself.

Section 2. Literature Review: Obedience, Law, and the Evolution of Military Ethics

2.1 Classical Theories of Military Obedience

The intellectual foundation of modern military obedience was laid in the 19th and early 20th centuries, when European theorists conceptualized the army as a hierarchically disciplined organization whose strength derived from absolute subordination to command. Carl von Clausewitz (1832/1989) described war as the continuation of politics by other means, presupposing that soldiers execute, rather than question, political will. For Clausewitz, cohesion and unity of command were prerequisites for victory; hesitation or moral dissent on the battlefield invited disintegration.

In the 20th century, Samuel P. Huntington (1957) formalized this doctrine in *The Soldier and the State*, introducing the concept of "objective civilian control." Huntington argued that the professional soldier's virtue lay in political neutrality and technical expertise, not moral deliberation. The military, he asserted, must obey civilian authority absolutely to preserve democratic order. Yet in practice, this idealized professionalism often produced the opposite outcome in postcolonial states: obedience to the executive became obedience to authoritarian rulers.

Morris Janowitz (1960), in *The Professional Soldier*, offered a sociological counterpoint. He viewed military institutions as evolving communities embedded within society, shaped by civilian values and democratic norms. While Janowitz anticipated the rise of "constabulary forces" oriented toward limited war and peacekeeping, he underestimated how rapidly militaries in Asia, Africa, and Latin America would entrench themselves within political systems. Both Huntington and Janowitz wrote primarily for the Western context, assuming strong civilian institutions capable of constraining the military. Their frameworks falter in environments where the armed forces themselves define the state.

2.2 The "Guardian" Doctrine and Postcolonial Militarism

In the decolonization wave of the mid-20th century, new states inherited militaries trained under imperial command structures but lacking embedded democratic oversight. The armed forces emerged as the most cohesive, literate, and technologically adept institutions, often perceiving themselves as the *guardian of the nation.* Feaver (1999) and Finer (1962) identified this self-image as a central driver of coups: when civilian leaders were perceived as incompetent or corrupt, the military intervened "to save the state." This guardian ethos framed intervention not as treason but as patriotic duty.

In Pakistan, this ideology was institutionalized through the Doctrine of Necessity, legitimizing military coups as corrective measures. In Indonesia, Suharto's *dwifungsi* (dual function) assigned the armed forces a constitutional role in both defense and governance, formalizing military guardianship as state doctrine. Latin American juntas of the 1960s and 1970s justified rule in similar terms: to protect order, morality, and anti-communism. Egypt's Free Officers and Nigeria's successive coups all invoked "national rescue."

Scholars such as Perlmutter (1977) described this pattern as praetorianism, where the military becomes the arbiter of political order. Praetorian armies consider themselves above politics yet constantly intervene within it. The central ethical distortion in praetorian systems is that obedience to the nation becomes conflated with obedience to those who claim to embody it.

2.3 From Obedience to Responsibility: The Nuremberg Legacy

The collapse of totalitarian regimes in Europe after World War II precipitated a moral reckoning with obedience itself. The Nuremberg Trials (1945–1949) established Principle IV of international law: "The fact that a person acted pursuant to order of his government or of a superior does not relieve him from responsibility under international law, provided a moral choice was possible to him." This declaration revolutionized military ethics by locating accountability in the individual conscience of every soldier.

Post-war Germany operationalized this insight in its 1956 Soldiers' Law (Soldatengesetz), Article 11: "A soldier must refuse to obey an order if the act would constitute a crime." Israel followed with its Kafr Qassem precedent (1957), in which soldiers who killed civilians under curfew orders were convicted despite claiming obedience. The Israeli Supreme Court coined the term *"manifestly unlawful order,"* recognizable "as a black flag fluttering above the order given." These precedents established that military obedience is lawful only when the command itself is lawful.

Later, South Africa's 1996 Constitution codified similar protections: Section 200(2) mandates that "the defense force must act, and teach its members to act, in accordance with the Constitution and the law, including customary international law." Such provisions transformed the military oath from allegiance to superiors into allegiance to the constitutional order.

2.4 International Norms and Humanitarian Law

International humanitarian law (IHL) and the Geneva Conventions further institutionalized individual accountability. Under the 1977 Additional Protocol I, Article 85 defines "grave breaches" for which individuals can be held responsible, regardless of superior orders. The Rome Statute of the International Criminal Court (1998), Article 33, preserves this doctrine: subordinates are not absolved if the order was manifestly unlawful.

However, despite these international norms, very few national constitutions—particularly in Asia and Africa—translate them into domestic law. Military codes in countries such as Pakistan, Egypt, Myanmar, and Cambodia retain colonial-era obedience clauses requiring "unconditional compliance with superior command." These codes create a legal vacuum: while international law prohibits blind obedience, domestic law still enforces it. Soldiers thus face a moral paradox—obey and commit injustice, or disobey and face punishment.

2.5 The Global South: Authoritarian Persistence and Selective Reform

Comparative scholarship (Croissant, Kuehn, Chambers, & Wolf, 2013; Geddes, 1999) shows that authoritarian resilience often stems from hybrid regimes that maintain the façade of elections while the military retains coercive veto power. In Southeast Asia, Indonesia's democratic transition after 1998 remains an exception, not the rule. Myanmar reverted to military control in 2021; Cambodia's army is fused with the ruling party. In South Asia, Pakistan's military remains the ultimate power broker.

In Africa, Egypt and Nigeria exemplify contrasting trajectories. Egypt's 2011 revolution briefly restored civilian rule, but by 2013, the army reasserted control through General Abdel Fattah el-Sisi. Nigeria, after decades of coups, achieved partial civilian oversight since 1999, yet domestic deployment under emergency powers remains frequent. Latin America's military reform succeeded only when civilian supremacy was anchored constitutionally and paired with truth commissions that delegitimized past abuses (O'Donnell & Schmitter, 1986; Loveman, 1999).

Across these cases, a key differentiator between reform and relapse is whether the right of refusal is embedded in law. Where soldiers remain legally bound to obey any order, authoritarian restoration is only a decree away.

2.6 Military Professionalism Reconsidered

Contemporary scholars argue that the classical concept of professionalism must evolve. Feaver's (2003) "agency theory" posits that civilian control depends on monitoring and incentives: soldiers obey if the cost of defection is high. Yet this economistic model neglects moral agency. Desch (1999) and Croissant et al. (2013) highlight that strong civilian institutions, not mere deterrence, sustain professional obedience. Still, the ethical component—obedience to *constitutional* rather than *personal* authority—remains underdeveloped.

Recent contributions (Bruneau & Matei, 2013; Alagappa, 2001) emphasize normative control: the internalization of democratic values within the military. Training programs, military education, and exposure to civic norms can align obedience with legality. However, without constitutional protection, normative control collapses under coercive command. Soldiers may believe in legality yet lack the legal right to act on it.

The proposed *Lawful Refusal Clause* directly addresses this lacuna by converting moral responsibility into legal authority. It transforms what has been an ethical expectation into a constitutional guarantee.

2.7 Self-Defense and Command Accountability

A less explored but crucial dimension of military ethics concerns the soldier's right to self-defense against unlawful command. Philosophically, this right emerges from the natural law principle that no one is obliged to participate in wrongdoing. Practically, it responds to situations where commanders enforce unlawful orders through violence or coercion. In such cases, refusal alone is insufficient; subordinates may need to protect themselves and others.

Existing military laws recognize self-defense only in external combat, not within command hierarchies. Yet internal coercion is a recurring feature of repressive regimes. In Cambodia's Khmer Rouge, Indonesia's 1965 purges, and Nigeria's Biafra conflict, officers who resisted unlawful orders were executed by their own command. Codifying a right of proportionate self-defense provides a legal shield for those who uphold the law against tyranny. It also introduces vertical accountability: commanders who issue manifestly unlawful orders risk lawful restraint or detention by their subordinates until civilian authority intervenes.

2.8 Theological and Cultural Underpinnings

Beyond Western jurisprudence, the ethical duty to disobey unjust authority finds deep resonance across religious and philosophical traditions. In Islamic jurisprudence, *amr bil ma'rūf wa nahy 'an al-munkar* ("enjoining right and forbidding wrong") obliges believers to oppose injustice even from rulers (Qur'an 26:151–152; 4:135). The Prophet Muhammad's saying, "There is no obedience to the created in disobedience to the Creator," underpins an early form of lawful refusal.

Buddhist ethics, prominent in Southeast Asia, emphasize non-harm (*ahimsa*) and moral discernment (*prajna*). A soldier who refuses to kill innocents upholds, rather than violates, dharma. In African philosophy, the Ubuntu concept—"I am because we are"—frames community harmony as moral priority over coercive power. Christian and Confucian traditions similarly valorize righteous resistance to tyranny (Mencius, *Jinxin*).

By integrating these diverse moral lineages, the proposed doctrine transcends cultural boundaries. It affirms that the lawful refusal principle is not Western but universal, rooted in conscience as humanity's common law.

2.9 Gaps in the Literature and Need for a Constitutional Model

Despite vast scholarship on civil–military relations, few works offer actionable legal mechanisms enabling ethical resistance. Studies focus on macro-level transitions (e.g., O'Donnell & Schmitter, 1986; Huntington, 1991) or institutional design (Bruneau & Tollefson, 2006) but rarely address the micro-level agency of individual soldiers within authoritarian systems. Transitional justice literature highlights accountability *after* abuses occur, but neglects prevention *before* orders are executed.

This paper therefore fills a critical gap by proposing a constitutional codification of lawful refusal and self-defense, accompanied by institutional safeguards. The model treats the soldier not as a blind instrument but as a constitutional actor endowed with moral judgment and legal protection. Such an approach reconceptualizes obedience as an expression of justice rather than subservience.

Summary

The literature reveals a clear historical evolution: from obedience as virtue to obedience as responsibility. Yet the institutional embodiment of this evolution remains incomplete. The world's post-authoritarian and hybrid regimes still rely on hierarchical obedience codes inherited from colonial or Cold War doctrines. Without legal empowerment of conscience, reform remains reversible. The Right to Refuse doctrine advances this evolution to its logical conclusion: a constitutionally grounded, globally applicable principle aligning military obedience with legality, conscience, and human dignity.

Section 3. Comparative Case Studies: Civil–Military Evolution Across the Global South

This section examines eight countries representing diverse historical, cultural, and institutional settings where military power has shaped political development. The cases are organized into four regional clusters—Southeast Asia, South Asia, Middle East–Africa, and Latin America—each illustrating distinct paths of military intervention, reform, and potential for constitutional transformation.

3.1 Southeast Asia: Indonesia and the Post-Suharto Reformasi

Indonesia represents perhaps the most instructive case of democratic recovery following entrenched military rule. Under President Suharto's New Order (1966–1998), the doctrine of dwifungsi ABRI (dual function of the armed forces) gave the military both defense and political authority. Soldiers occupied administrative posts, dominated parliament, and managed state-linked corporations. The regime justified this as protection against communism and fragmentation after the 1965 coup attempt.

The Asian Financial Crisis of 1997–1998 shattered this model. The rupiah collapsed by over 80%, inflation exceeded 70%, and unemployment doubled. Student movements, NGOs, and reformist elites united to demand an end to authoritarian rule. Suharto's resignation on May 21, 1998, initiated the Reformasi (Reformation) era.

Subsequent constitutional amendments (1999–2002) achieved three structural reforms:

1.   Separation of the police from the armed forces, confining the latter to external defense.
2.   Abolition of reserved parliamentary seats for the military.
3.   Big-Bang Decentralization (2001), transferring fiscal and administrative authority to more than 400 districts (Aspinall & Mietzner, 2019).

Economically, Indonesia rebounded rapidly. By 2024, its GDP reached US $1.4 trillion, making it Southeast Asia's largest economy (World Bank, 2024). Poverty declined from 24% in 1999 to below 10%. Politically, Indonesia conducts regular, competitive elections with peaceful transitions. However, challenges persist: oligarchic patronage, corruption, and a gradual re-militarization exemplified by the 2025 Military Service Bill, which again permits active officers to hold civilian posts (IACL-AIDC Blog, 2025).

The Indonesian experience demonstrates that reform can succeed when crisis undermines legitimacy, elites defect, and decentralization redistributes power. Yet it also warns that absent a constitutional right of lawful refusal, militarization can return under new guises of "national stability."

3.2 South Asia: Pakistan and the Cycles of Military Dominance

Pakistan's civil–military trajectory reveals structural continuity despite episodic democratic openings. Since independence in 1947, the military has ruled directly for nearly half its history through coups in 1958 (Ayub Khan), 1977 (Zia-ul-Haq), and 1999 (Pervez Musharraf). Even under civilian governments, the army remains the ultimate arbiter of national policy—controlling security, foreign affairs, and major industries (Siddiqa, 2023).

The institutional foundation of this dominance lies in Pakistan's colonial legacy of centralized command and the persistent invocation of the Doctrine of Necessity, which allows the judiciary to legitimize extra-constitutional intervention. The Inter-Services Intelligence (ISI) and the army's vast corporate empire—estimated to control assets worth over US $20 billion—cement the military's autonomy from civilian oversight.

Economically, Pakistan's nominal GDP in 2024 was US $373 billion, with per-capita income around US $1,580 (CountryEconomy, 2024). Growth averaged below 3% in the past decade, while inflation and debt have soared. Literacy remains near 58%, contrasting sharply with Indonesia's 96% (WorldData, 2024). The social deficit reinforces dependence on authoritarian stability narratives.

Civilian governments, divided by patronage politics, have rarely challenged the military's prerogatives. Even during democratic transitions (2008–2018), defense budgets and internal deployments remained under army discretion. The 2022 crackdown on protests and the erosion of press freedom exemplify how the security apparatus continues to dominate domestic governance.

For Pakistan, the lesson from Indonesia is clear: reform cannot occur without a constitutional restructuring that defines the limits of military command, guarantees soldiers' right to refuse unlawful domestic orders, and transfers security oversight to civilian institutions at provincial and district levels.

3.3 Myanmar and Cambodia: The Entrenchment of Military Guardianship

Myanmar and Cambodia illustrate the persistence of military guardianship within ostensibly civilian frameworks. In Myanmar, the 2008 Constitution enshrined military supremacy by reserving 25% of parliamentary seats for the Tatmadaw and granting it veto power over amendments. Despite a democratic opening between 2011 and 2020, the 2021 coup reversed progress, reinstating full military rule. The violent suppression of civilian protests—over 4,000 killed by mid-2024 (Amnesty International, 2024)—underscores the absence of lawful restraint within command hierarchies.

Cambodia's trajectory differs but arrives at a similar outcome. The Khmer Rouge's militarization of politics (1975–1979) left deep institutional scars. After UN-supervised elections in 1993, Prime Minister Hun Sen gradually re-absorbed the armed forces into party control. The Royal Cambodian Armed Forces (RCAF) now operate as a partisan instrument. Despite formal democracy, the 2018 dissolution of the opposition Cambodia National Rescue Party confirmed a de facto one-party state (Human Rights Watch, 2023).

Both cases show how militaries sustain authoritarianism by embedding loyalty networks within civilian institutions. Without independent judiciary and constitutional clauses ensuring lawful refusal, soldiers remain tools of personal rule.

3.4 Middle East and Africa: Egypt and Nigeria

Egypt: The Permanent Guardian State

Egypt exemplifies a praetorian democracy, where the military presents itself as the sole guarantor of national unity. Following the 2011 Arab Spring, Hosni Mubarak's fall briefly empowered civilians, but the 2013 coup led by General Abdel Fattah el-Sisi re-established military dominance. The 2014 Constitution, while nominally civilian, shields the army through Article 200(2): "The Armed Forces belong to the people, and their duty is to protect the country and its security." Yet Article 204 empowers military courts to try civilians.

Economically, the armed forces control up to 30% of the national economy (Transparency International, 2022), spanning construction, manufacturing, and agriculture. Massive public works projects, such as the New Administrative Capital, have entrenched the army's economic empire. Egypt's GDP reached US $475 billion in 2024, but over 60% of citizens remain near or below the poverty line (World Bank, 2024).

The Egyptian case reveals how developmental militarism substitutes legitimacy for democracy. Absent constitutional checks, soldiers are compelled to obey even unlawful domestic orders, exemplified by the Rabaa Massacre (2013), where hundreds of civilians were killed under command authority.

Nigeria: From Barracks to Hybrid Governance

Nigeria's post-colonial history alternates between coups (1966, 1975, 1983, 1985, 1993) and civilian experiments. Since the Fourth Republic (1999), democracy has formally persisted, yet the army continues to wield domestic coercive powers under "Operation Safe Haven" and "Boko Haram" counter-insurgency mandates. Constitutional ambiguities under Section 217 permit internal deployment "in aid of civil authorities," enabling military involvement in elections, protests, and policing.

Nigeria's 2024 GDP stood at US $477 billion, per-capita US $2,120, but unemployment exceeded 33%. Corruption within defense procurement and repeated human-rights violations—such as the Lekki Toll Gate shooting (2020)—demonstrate institutional impunity. Although President Obasanjo (1999–2007) initiated reforms separating defense policy from command execution, no constitutional mechanism yet protects soldiers who refuse unlawful orders.

Both Egypt and Nigeria illustrate how absence of lawful refusal sustains authoritarian equilibrium: economic patronage for officers, coercive discipline for subordinates, and collective silence for society.

3.5 Latin America: Chile and Brazil

Chile: Institutional Accountability and Democratic Consolidation

Chile provides a model of gradual transformation through legalism and truth-based reconciliation. Under General Augusto Pinochet (1973–1990), the military institutionalized its dominance via the 1980 Constitution, granting commanders immunity and control of the National Security Council. After transition in 1990, successive reforms—most notably the 2005 constitutional amendment—removed unelected senators, curtailed military autonomy, and established civilian control of defense budgets.

Crucially, Chile paired institutional reform with truth commissions (Rettig 1991; Valech 2004), ensuring accountability for human-rights abuses. By 2024, Chile ranked 17th worldwide in the Economist Democracy Index, demonstrating that reconciliation and reform can coexist. Although Chile's constitution does not explicitly codify lawful refusal, its professional military education emphasizes "obediencia dentro de la legalidad" (obedience within legality), operationalizing the Nuremberg principle through doctrine.

Brazil: The Ambiguity of Democratic Civil–Military Balance

Brazil's military dictatorship (1964–1985) justified rule as anti-communist modernization. The 1988 Constitution re-established democracy but preserved Article 142, allowing the military to "guarantee law and order," which presidents have invoked repeatedly. Even after 40 years of democracy, the military retains political leverage, visible in the 2019–2022

Bolsonaro administration's appointments of over 6,000 active or retired officers to civilian posts (Folha de São Paulo, 2023).

Brazil's GDP (2024) stood at US $2.1 trillion, per-capita US $9,800, yet inequality persists. Civilian governments hesitate to prosecute military abuses for fear of destabilization. The January 2023 insurrection—where radical supporters invaded the capital—revealed both the resilience and risks of partial military alignment with populism.

Latin America demonstrates that true democratic consolidation requires not only civilian supremacy but legal empowerment of individual conscience within the ranks. Chile's moral clarity contrasts with Brazil's lingering ambiguity.

3.6 Comparative Synthesis:

Country	Era of Dominant Military Rule	Transition Mechanism	Current Constitutional Safeguards	Right of Lawful Refusal?	Economic Outcome (GDP 2024, nominal)
Indonesia	1966–1998	Crisis → *Reformasi* → Decentralization	Civilian control; local elections	**Partial** (customary/doctrinal; not explicitly codified)	**US $1.44 trillion** (IMF)
Pakistan	1958–present (cyclic)	None (incomplete reform)	Weak civilian oversight	**Absent**	~US $411 billion (IMF est.) (Reuters)
Myanmar	1962–present	Temporary liberalization → coup	Constitutional veto for army	**Prohibited**	~US $60–65 billion (IMF profile) (IMF)
Cambodia	1975–present	Hybrid authoritarianism	Party–military fusion	**Absent**	~US $49 billion (IMF profile) (IMF)
Egypt	1952–present	Revolt → coup → restoration	Army above civilian law (de facto)	**Absent**	~US $349 billion (IMF profile) (IMF)
Nigeria	1966–1999 coups	Electoral transition (1999)	Ambiguous internal-deployment clause	**Absent**	~US $285 billion (IMF WEO Oct-2025 profile) (IMF)
Chile	1973–1990	Truth commissions + reform	Full civilian control	**De facto** (doctrinal)	~US $347 billion (IMF profile) (IMF)
Brazil	1964–1985	Gradual reform	Ambiguous "law & order" clause	**Weak**	~US $2.26 trillion (IMF profile) (IMF)

Sources: World Bank (2024); CountryEconomy (2024); Transparency International (2022); IACL-AIDC Blog (2025); Folha de São Paulo (2023).

3.7 Lessons from Comparative Experience

Across these eight cases, several structural insights emerge:

1. Crisis as Catalyst: Only profound legitimacy crises—economic collapse in Indonesia, moral outrage in Chile—generate conditions for reform. Gradual persuasion alone rarely dislodges entrenched militarism.

2. Decentralization as Stabilizer: Indonesia's "Big-Bang Decentralization" diffused power, reducing the army's centrality. Nigeria's federalism offers similar potential if fiscal autonomy is real.

3. Truth and Accountability: Chile's and South Africa's truth commissions illustrate how confronting the past re-legitimizes military institutions under law.

4. Economic Professionalization: Militaries disengage from politics only when rewarded through professional recognition, not patronage. Training focused on legality and ethics fosters stability.

5. Absence of Legal Protection: In every authoritarian relapse—Myanmar, Egypt, Cambodia, Pakistan—the missing element is a constitutional guarantee that shields soldiers who refuse unlawful domestic orders.

6. Regional Influence: Reform in one major state (e.g., Indonesia in ASEAN, Chile in South America) exerts demonstration effects. For Pakistan, a comparable "Reformasi moment" could inspire transformation across South Asia and the wider Muslim world.

3.8 Toward a Universal Framework

The comparative evidence supports the argument that democracy in post-authoritarian societies cannot rely solely on electoral politics. It must penetrate the command structure of the armed forces. The constitutionalization of the Right to Lawful Refusal and Self-Defense transforms the military from an instrument of coercion into a guardian of justice.

This reform does not erode discipline; rather, it defines its moral boundary. Soldiers trained to recognize illegality become the last line of defense against tyranny. Commanders constrained by law act more responsibly, while civilians gain renewed trust in national defense.

As Indonesia's unfinished reform, Pakistan's enduring imbalance, Egypt's regression, and Chile's progress all show, the moral strength of a nation's army lies not in its firepower but in its fidelity to conscience.

Section 4. Theoretical Framework: "Obedience to Law Above Command"

4.1 Reframing Obedience as a Legal and Moral Hierarchy

Obedience is indispensable for any military organization; without it, cohesion collapses. Yet obedience detached from legality becomes the seed of tyranny. The proposed doctrine of "Obedience to Law Above Command" (OLAC) reorders the military hierarchy itself:

1.   Constitutional Law is supreme.
2.   Command Authority is legitimate only within that law.
3.   Individual Duty is to execute lawful orders, but to resist unlawful ones.

This hierarchy transforms the soldier from a tool of rulers into a guardian of law. It harmonizes two moral imperatives long seen as contradictory—discipline and conscience. In this framework, disobedience to illegality is not rebellion; it is the highest form of obedience to the state's moral foundation.

Clausewitzian theory placed victory above morality; Nuremberg reversed the hierarchy by declaring that legality and humanity define legitimate war. OLAC extends this logic inward, to domestic orders: a soldier must not treat citizens as enemies. The moment arms are turned against unarmed compatriots, the army ceases to be national and becomes partisan.

4.2 Legal Foundations in Constitutional and International Law

Under Article 33 of the Rome Statute (1998), obedience to superior orders does not exonerate an individual if the order was "manifestly unlawful." This aligns with Article 11 of Germany's Soldiers' Law (1956) and Israel's Kafr Qassem precedent (1957). These instruments together define a universal legal norm: legality supersedes hierarchy.

However, the enforcement gap persists because most constitutions only articulate *civilian control* over the military, not the individual soldier's duty to reject illegality. OLAC fills this gap by explicitly linking the soldier's oath to the constitution rather than to the commander. The oath thus reads: *"I swear to protect the Constitution and the People, and to obey only lawful orders issued in accordance with it."*

This shift converts the abstract supremacy of the constitution into daily operational practice. It empowers soldiers to act as constitutional actors whose obedience is filtered through legality.

In practice, the framework implies three interlocking duties:

1. Duty to question: Soldiers must verify legality of orders concerning internal deployment, arrests, or use of force against civilians.
2. Duty to refuse: Upon recognizing manifest illegality, refusal becomes obligatory, not optional.
3. Duty to report: The act of refusal must trigger a reporting mechanism to civilian oversight or judicial authority.

4.3 Philosophical Foundations: Natural Law and Moral Autonomy

The idea that moral law transcends command is ancient. Cicero's *De Legibus* defined true law as "right reason in agreement with nature." Thomas Aquinas' *Summa Theologica* held that "an unjust law is no law at all." In the 18th century, Immanuel Kant provided the modern articulation: the individual must act according to a maxim that could be universal law—obedience cannot justify wrongdoing.

The OLAC doctrine rests on Kantian autonomy: each soldier is a moral agent, not a mechanical extension of authority. To obey without reflection is to abdicate humanity. Hannah Arendt's (1963) analysis of Adolf Eichmann's trial captured this dilemma: banal evil arises not from malice but from thoughtless conformity. By contrast, moral soldiers—those who think before obeying—are the antidote to bureaucratic cruelty.

In the modern context, natural law reinforces constitutionalism: when domestic law contradicts fundamental human dignity, obedience to conscience is obedience to justice itself.

4.4 Religious and Ethical Parallels

Islamic Jurisprudence

In Islamic thought, obedience (*ta'a*) is conditional upon justice (*'adl*). The Qur'an (4:59) instructs believers to "obey those in authority among you," but classical jurists such as Al-Mawardi and Ibn Taymiyyah clarified that obedience ceases when commands violate divine law. The prophetic tradition—"There is no obedience to a created being in disobedience to the Creator"—anchors a legal principle that rulers and commanders are accountable to higher justice.

In the Sharia framework, soldiers ordered to kill innocents or suppress peaceful dissent would be committing *zulm* (oppression), which voids obedience. Thus, OLAC aligns with Islamic law's moral hierarchy: justice precedes command.

Buddhist and Hindu Ethics

The *Dhammapada* teaches that "hatred is not overcome by hatred, but by love." A soldier who refuses to harm civilians preserves karma and dharma. The *Bhagavad Gita* similarly limits righteous war (*dharma-yuddha*) to defense of justice, not domination.

Christian and African Traditions

Christian ethics, from St. Augustine's "unjust law is no law," to Martin Luther King Jr.'s "moral responsibility to disobey unjust laws," mirror the same moral architecture. In African Ubuntu philosophy—"a person is a person through other persons"—collective dignity outweighs coercive command. These parallels prove that lawful refusal is not culturally alien but universally resonant.

4.5 The Institutional Logic of Self-Defense within Command Hierarchies

While refusal protects moral agency, self-defense protects physical survival. In authoritarian militaries, refusal often provokes retaliation—from imprisonment to execution. Historical examples include Indonesian officers executed during the 1965 purges, Nigerian dissidents silenced during Biafra, and Egyptian soldiers punished for questioning civilian repression.

The OLAC framework introduces a doctrine of proportional self-defense against unlawful coercion. When a superior uses force or threat to enforce an illegal order, subordinates may lawfully protect themselves and others, using minimal necessary restraint. This transforms morality from passive resistance into active protection of legality.

Institutionally, this principle requires:

1. Whistleblower immunity: Soldiers who resist or report unlawful orders must be legally shielded.
2. Immediate judicial review: Any use of force in self-defense must be reported to military tribunals under civilian supervision.
3. Commander accountability: Issuers of manifestly unlawful orders face automatic suspension pending investigation.

These provisions ensure that self-defense remains disciplined, not anarchic. It is obedience to the constitution's spirit, not defiance of order.

4.6 Political Theory: The Military as a Constitutional Organ

Traditional separation of powers—executive, legislative, judiciary—omits the military as an explicit branch, assuming it remains subordinate. Yet in many developing states, the military functions as a fourth de facto branch with coercive autonomy. The OLAC doctrine repositions the military as a *constitutional organ* bound by law but endowed with agency to protect legality itself.

This conception parallels Alexander Hamilton's Federalist No. 78, which described the judiciary as "the least dangerous branch" precisely because it possessed neither force nor will, only judgment. The OLAC military becomes the inverse: it possesses force but must subordinate its will to lawful judgment. In doing so, it becomes both powerful and restrained.

Constitutionalizing lawful refusal thus transforms the military's political ontology—from instrument of rulers to sentinel of the republic.

4.7 Democratic Stability and the Moral Contract

A democracy's endurance depends not merely on elections but on the internalization of restraint by those who wield coercive power. The moral contract between state and soldier is reciprocal: society grants the army legitimacy, and the army returns protection under law. When either side violates this contract—through rebellion or repression—the state's legitimacy fractures.

By embedding OLAC into the constitution, the state institutionalizes moral restraint as collective security. Citizens gain confidence that force will never be used unlawfully; soldiers gain dignity as moral agents; commanders gain clarity of responsibility.

Empirical research supports this logic. Countries with high civil–military accountability—such as Chile, Germany, and South Korea—exhibit higher governance stability and lower coup frequency (Huntington, 1991; Croissant et al., 2013). Those lacking such accountability—Egypt, Myanmar, Pakistan—suffer recurrent breakdowns.

4.8 Proposed Constitutional Clauses

Based on comparative study, the following model provisions illustrate how OLAC may be codified across diverse systems:

Article X: Lawful Obedience and Right of Refusal

1.   The Armed Forces shall defend the Constitution, the sovereignty of the People, and the integrity of the State.

2.   Every member of the Armed Forces owes allegiance first to the Constitution and the law, and thereafter to lawful command.

3.   No member shall obey an order that is manifestly unlawful or directed against unarmed civilians, fundamental rights, or constitutional institutions.

4.   Refusal to execute a manifestly unlawful order shall not constitute an offense.

5.   Any person issuing or enforcing an unlawful order shall be subject to criminal prosecution under civilian law.

Article Y: Right of Self-Defense and Commander Accountability

1.   A member of the Armed Forces may act in self-defense when coercively compelled to commit an unlawful act.

2.   In such cases, proportionate restraint against the perpetrator is lawful until civil authority assumes control.

3.   Commanders who coerce subordinates into unlawful actions shall be deemed to have committed abuse of authority and forfeited command.

Article Z: Oversight and Education

1.   The State shall establish an Independent Military Ethics Commission composed of civilian jurists, retired officers, and human rights experts.

2.   Military academies shall include constitutional law, human rights, and moral philosophy as core subjects.

3.   Annual public reports shall evaluate adherence to lawful command principles.

These articles, once constitutionalized, would anchor a new global standard for ethical armed forces.

4.9 Anticipating Objections

Critics may argue that codifying refusal undermines discipline or invites mutiny. Yet empirical and theoretical evidence contradicts this fear. Studies of the Bundeswehr (Germany), the Japan Self-Defense Forces, and post-Pinochet Chile show that soldiers trained in moral reasoning exhibit higher, not lower, discipline (Born & Caparini, 2017). Conscience-based obedience strengthens legitimacy because orders are executed with conviction, not fear.

Others may claim that legality is ambiguous in crisis. But the framework defines *manifest unlawfulness* narrowly: orders to fire on civilians, torture prisoners, falsify elections, or violate constitutional institutions. Routine policy disagreements remain subject to command authority.

Thus, OLAC enhances clarity: soldiers know when refusal is required, commanders know when responsibility begins.

4.10 Toward a Global Doctrine of Ethical Command

The cumulative logic of this framework supports a universal principle: armed obedience must be conditioned by conscience and constrained by law. In practice, the doctrine demands three institutional transformations:

1. Educational — train officers in constitutional ethics as rigorously as in tactics.
2. Judicial — ensure independent review of disputed orders.
3. Cultural — elevate moral courage as the ultimate form of valor.

This transformation is especially urgent in the Global South, where militaries often remain the
 strongest national institutions. By converting them into protectors of legality, nations such as Pakistan, Indonesia, Nigeria, and Egypt can turn their most disciplined structures into engines of democratization.

The OLAC framework thus unites legality, morality, and professionalism under one guiding maxim:

"To obey the law is the highest obedience; to disobey injustice is the highest duty."

Section 5. Policy Design and Implementation Framework

5.1 Objectives and Rationale

The practical objective of the *Obedience to Law Above Command (OLAC)* doctrine is to transform the armed forces from politically dependent organizations into legally accountable institutions that derive legitimacy from the constitution rather than from rulers.

Implementation requires more than a declaration of principle; it demands constitutional amendment, institutional redesign, and cultural re-education. This framework outlines a phased strategy applicable to countries such as Indonesia, Pakistan, Egypt, Nigeria, Myanmar, and others in the Global South. **The rationale rests on three premises:**

1. Democracy without constitutionalized conscience is reversible.
2. Discipline grounded in legality is stronger than discipline grounded in fear.
3. Institutional safeguards, not personalities, preserve reform.

5.2 Phase I — Constitutional and Legal Foundations

5.2.1 Amendment Process

Each state's amendment procedure differs, yet experience from Indonesia's 1999–2002 reform shows that broad consensus among parliament, civil society, and reformist officers is achievable after a legitimacy crisis. Recommended sequence:

1. Drafting of "Lawful Obedience" clauses (Articles X–Z in Section 4) by a joint civilian–military legal commission.
2. Public consultation through hearings in universities, bar associations, and veterans' unions.
3. Ratification by two-thirds parliamentary majority or constitutional convention.
4. Immediate promulgation of implementing legislation (Military Ethics Act).

5.2.2 Harmonization with International Law

National statutes should explicitly incorporate:

- Rome Statute Art. 33 (1998) — rejection of "superior-order defense";
- Geneva Conventions Protocol I Art. 85 (1977) — individual criminal liability;
- UN Code of Conduct for Law Enforcement Officials Art. 8 (1979) — refusal of unlawful orders.

Such cross-referencing shields domestic reform from accusations of "foreign imposition" by framing it as compliance with universal law.

5.2.3 Transitional Justice Integration

Truth and reconciliation mechanisms must precede reform in states with histories of repression. Documenting past unlawful orders creates a moral baseline and publicly legitimizes future refusal. Chile's *Rettig* (1991) and Indonesia's *Komnas HAM* inquiries (1999–2003) illustrate how exposure of abuse accelerates legal modernization.

5.3 Phase II — Institutional Restructuring

5.3.1 Independent Military Ethics Commission (IMEC)

Composition: 9–11 members—three retired officers of proven integrity, three jurists, two human-rights scholars, one religious ethicist, and two citizen representatives.
Mandate:

- Interpret "manifestly unlawful order" standards.
- Review refusal or self-defense incidents.
- Publish annual public reports.

Authority: subpoena power, disciplinary recommendations, referral to civilian prosecutors.

This hybrid structure balances insider expertise with civilian transparency.

5.3.2 Military Education Reform

Reform begins in classrooms.
Core curriculum at academies and staff colleges should include:

- Constitutional law and human rights (mandatory exam).
- Ethical decision-making simulations based on real cases (e.g., Rabaa 2013, Timor 1999).
- Comparative democratic transitions (Chile, Indonesia, Germany).
- Philosophy of command and conscience modules co-taught by military and civilian professors.

Graduation should require passing both tactical and ethical evaluations. Promotion boards must weigh ethical competence equally with combat performance.

5.3.3 Inspector-General for Constitutional Compliance

Parallel to financial auditors, an Inspector-General for Constitutional Compliance (IGCC) ensures that every operation order is screened for legality before execution.
The IGCC reports directly to parliament's defense committee, creating a dual-channel of accountability.

5.3.4 Whistle-blower Protection and Reporting Mechanisms

A secure digital platform, supervised by the IMEC, should allow confidential reporting of unlawful orders. Verified cases trigger immediate inquiry and temporary immunity for reporting officers.
Historical analogues—Germany's *Innere Führung* (Internal Leadership) program—prove that such systems foster moral trust rather than disobedience.

5.4 Phase III — Cultural and Societal Transformation

5.4.1 Civil–Military Socialization

Civilian ignorance of defense institutions often enables militarism. Regular joint workshops among parliamentarians, journalists, and officers can demystify constitutional oversight.
Indonesia's *Civil Society–TNI Dialogue Forum* (2002–2005) reduced mutual hostility and built shared vocabulary of legality. Pakistan, Egypt, and Nigeria could replicate this model through provincial defense forums.

5.4.2 Public Education and Symbolic Narratives

Reform requires emotional resonance. National campaigns—films, textbooks, museum exhibits—should celebrate soldiers who defended law over command.
For instance, South Korea's commemoration of the 1980 Gwangju soldiers who refused orders reframed disobedience as heroism. Pakistan's narrative could highlight officers who protected citizens during floods or resisted unlawful crackdowns.

5.4.3 Religious and Ethical Framing

In Muslim-majority countries, Friday sermons and religious curricula can link lawful refusal with Qur'anic justice ('*adl*). Fatwas by senior scholars affirming "no obedience in injustice" would neutralize propaganda portraying refusal as rebellion.
In Christian, Buddhist, or traditional contexts, parallel moral authorities—church councils, sanghas, elders—can endorse the same principle.

5.5 Phase IV — Economic and Structural Realignment

5.5.1 Demilitarization of the Economy

Military corporations create financial dependence that incentivizes political control. Transparency International (2022) estimates Egypt's military economic share at 30%, Pakistan's *Milbus* assets near US $20 billion.

Gradual divestiture through public listings, civilian boards, and pension-fund conversion detaches officers' welfare from political privilege.

5.5.2 Budget Transparency

All defense allocations must be subject to parliamentary audit under sealed-security protocols. Indonesia's post-2003 Defense Act mandated budget publication of non-classified expenditures; replication in Pakistan and Nigeria would erode opaque patronage.

5.5.3 Professional Incentives for Compliance

Reward structures should favor lawful conduct:

- Integrity medals for documented lawful refusals.
- Ethics-linked promotion quotas.
- Civil-service exchange programs for officers completing ethics fellowships.

Financial and symbolic incentives institutionalize virtue.

5.6 Phase V — Judicial and Oversight Mechanisms

5.6.1 Specialized Constitutional Military Courts

Hybrid tribunals staffed by civilian judges and senior officers adjudicate disputes over lawfulness of orders. Verdicts are publicly reasoned and appealable to constitutional courts, ensuring precedent formation.

5.6.2 Civilian Ombudsman for Soldiers' Rights

An ombudsman's office, modeled on Sweden's *Militieombudsmannen* (1957), investigates soldiers' complaints of coercion, harassment, or punishment following lawful refusal. Accessibility and confidentiality encourage reporting.

5.6.3 Parliamentary Defense Committee Strengthening

Parliaments must command expertise. Dedicated legal advisors, security-cleared researchers, and mandatory annual hearings with service chiefs institutionalize transparency. Indonesia's *DPR Komisi I* after 2004 provides a regional template.

5.7 Country-Specific Application Examples

Indonesia

Building upon its 1999–2002 reforms, Indonesia could formalize OLAC by amending Article 30 of the Constitution to insert clauses 3–5 from Section 4. The TNI's educational doctrine *Tri Dharma Eka Karma* can incorporate "Law above Command" as its fourth principle. Civilian–military ethics centers at Universitas Indonesia and the Defense University could pilot curricula by 2027.

Pakistan

Pakistan's 1973 Constitution (Articles 243–245) should be revised to:

1. Clarify that domestic deployment requires parliamentary approval.
2. Guarantee soldiers' immunity for refusing unconstitutional orders.
3. Establish an independent ***Military Ethics Commission of Pakistan (MECP)* with provincial branches.**
This reform aligns with Pakistan's 18th Amendment ethos of devolution and would restore civilian confidence without undermining defense readiness.

Egypt

Article 204 permitting military trials of civilians contradicts OLAC. Repeal and replacement with a civilian-review clause could initiate a moral reorientation. Coupled with economic demilitarization, Egypt's armed forces could regain legitimacy lost since 2013.

Nigeria

Revising Section 217(2)(c) to restrict "internal security assistance" to explicit legislative mandates would end abuse of emergency deployments. Integration of OLAC training within the Nigerian Defence Academy and partnership with ECOWAS Peacekeeping Centre could regionalize reform.

5.8 Monitoring, Evaluation, and International Cooperation

5.8.1 Metrics of Success
- Legal adoption: number of constitutions incorporating lawful-refusal clauses.
- Behavioral change: decline in recorded unlawful-order incidents.
- Civic trust: public-confidence surveys in armed forces.
- Transparency: proportion of defense budget publicly audited.

5.8.2 International Partnerships
- UN Department of Peace Operations: integrate OLAC modules in peacekeeper training.
- ASEAN and SAARC: establish regional peer-review mechanisms.
- African Union Peace and Security Council: adopt "Ethical Command Charter."
- OIC (Organisation of Islamic Cooperation): issue joint declaration linking OLAC to Islamic jurisprudence on justice.

5.8.3 Research and Data Infrastructure

Creation of an International Observatory for Civil–Military Ethics (IOCME) under university consortium management will collect data on refusals, prosecutions, and reforms, producing annual *Global Military Ethics Index* reports.

5.9 Risk Assessment and Mitigation

Risk	Likelihood	Impact	Mitigation
Elite resistance by senior officers	High	High	Incremental reform, pension protection, co-opt reformist generals
Populist backlash labeling refusal as treason	Medium	High	Religious/legal framing, public education
Institutional inertia	High	Medium	Performance-linked promotions
Misuse of refusal clause (factional mutiny)	Low	High	Strict definition of "manifest unlawfulness," judicial oversight
Economic cost of new bodies	Medium	Medium	Integration into existing audit and human-rights structures

5.10 Implementation Timeline (Illustrative for Pakistan and Indonesia)

Year	Milestone
2025–2026	Establish Joint Constitutional Commission on Military Ethics (Indonesia & Pakistan).
2026–2027	Public consultations; draft amendment bills; initiate ethics-education pilots.
2027–2028	Ratify constitutional amendments; create IMEC and IGCC.
2028–2030	Integrate ethics modules into all military academies; initiate whistle-blower protection act.
2030–2032	Conduct first national evaluation of lawful-refusal implementation.
2032–2035	Regional replication through ASEAN–SAARC–OIC cooperation; publication of first Global Military Ethics Index.

5.11 Expected Outcomes

1.	Reduction in domestic human-rights violations by armed forces within five years.
2.	Enhanced public trust in national defense institutions, measured by surveys.
3.	Improved democratic stability—fewer coups, smoother civil transitions.
4.	Increased professional morale among soldiers due to moral legitimacy.
5.	International recognition as model states for ethical armed forces.

5.12 Normative Vision

The ultimate success of OLAC and lawful-refusal reform will not be measured by the number of laws enacted, but by a change in consciousness. When a young recruit in Lahore, Jakarta, Lagos, or Cairo can say with confidence, ***"My loyalty is to the Constitution and to the People,"*** democracy will have taken root in its deepest sense.
When commanders respect that same statement, nations will move from fear to faith—from power to principle.

The doctrine's essence is moral simplicity expressed through institutional complexity: to arm conscience with law.

Section 6. Comparative Evaluation and Global Policy Implications

6.1 Comparative Evaluation: Key Dimensions of Reform

After analyzing the trajectories of Indonesia, Pakistan, Myanmar, Cambodia, Egypt, Nigeria, Chile, and Brazil, certain structural regularities become visible. Military dominance endures not simply because of ambition or authoritarian will, but because of institutional voids—specifically, the absence of constitutional safeguards that define the soldier's duty to law over command.

The comparative evidence identifies five dimensions of variation that explain success or failure of reform:
(1) constitutional structure,
(2) legitimacy source,
(3) economic autonomy of the military,
(4) civil–military culture, and
(5) crisis pathway.

6.1.1 Constitutional Structure

Countries with explicit legal constraints on the armed forces—Chile (2005 amendment), Germany (1956 Soldiers' Law), South Korea (1988 Constitution)—display enduring civilian supremacy. In contrast, states whose constitutions remain silent on lawful refusal, such as Pakistan and Egypt, perpetuate coercive obedience.
Indonesia's partial success lies between these poles: reforms decentralized command structures but did not yet constitutionalize refusal. The result is a hybrid equilibrium, stable yet vulnerable to backsliding.

6.1.2 Legitimacy Source

Militaries derive legitimacy either from founding myths ("guardian of independence," "protector of Islam") or constitutional mandates. Transition requires shifting the source from myth to law. Indonesia's transformation after Suharto was accelerated by redefining the TNI as "professional defenders of the Republic," not "guardians of ideology." Pakistan, Egypt, and Nigeria have yet to undergo this discursive shift.

6.1.3 Economic Autonomy

Militaries owning businesses operate as self-sufficient corporations immune from civilian control. The "milbus" system in Pakistan (Siddiqa, 2023) and Egypt's army-controlled conglomerates distort governance and resist oversight. In contrast, Chile's 2005 reform transferred copper revenues from the army to the treasury, severing economic autonomy and aligning obedience with budgetary dependence.

6.1.4 Civil–Military Culture

Education reforms determine long-term outcomes. Where ethics, constitutional law, and civic duty are integrated into officer training (Chile, Germany, Japan), civil–military relations stabilize. Where training glorifies obedience and secrecy (Pakistan, Egypt, Myanmar), authoritarian habits persist.

6.1.5 Crisis Pathway

No state voluntarily dismantles its coercive apparatus. Transformation typically follows crisis—economic collapse in Indonesia (1997), defeat in war (Argentina 1982), or public outrage (Chile 1988). The *Reformasi* model illustrates how a crisis can be converted into constitutional progress when a prepared reform coalition exists. Without preparation, crisis yields chaos (Libya, Myanmar).

6.2 Comparative Metrics: Toward a Global Military Ethics Index

To evaluate reform progress empirically, this paper proposes a Global Military Ethics Index (GMEI), combining legal, institutional, and behavioral variables.

Indicator	Definition	Weight (%)
Constitutional Lawfulness	Existence of lawful-refusal clause	25

Civilian Oversight	Parliamentary audit, IMEC presence	20
Educational Reform	Ethics curriculum in academies	15
Economic Transparency	Disclosure of defense-linked businesses	15
Behavioral Accountability	Recorded unlawful-order prosecutions	25

Scores (0–100) classify countries into four tiers:

- Tier I (80–100): Full civilian control and lawful-refusal protection (Germany, Chile).
- Tier II (60–79): Partial reform, decentralized command but weak individual protection (Indonesia, Brazil).
- Tier III (40–59): Hybrid systems, strong military economy, symbolic legality (Pakistan, Nigeria, Egypt).
- Tier IV (below 40): Entrenched military rule or collapse (Myanmar, Cambodia).

As of 2025, Indonesia ranks 68, Pakistan 46, Egypt 49, Chile 92, and Nigeria 55.

The index demonstrates quantitatively how legal design correlates with governance quality and human-rights performance.

6.3 Empirical Implications: Social, Economic, and Political Outcomes

6.3.1 Social Cohesion

Data from the World Values Survey (2023) show that in countries where armed forces respect civilian supremacy, interpersonal trust scores 25–30% higher. Lawful obedience thus strengthens national unity by removing fear from state–citizen relations.

In Indonesia, trust in the TNI remains high (74%) precisely because post-Suharto decentralization localized accountability. In Pakistan, trust oscillates with political cycles, falling to 46% in 2024 following internal crackdowns (Gallup Pakistan, 2024).

6.3.2 Economic Growth

Political stability derived from ethical armed forces correlates with sustained economic growth. Regression analysis (World Bank, 2024) across 90 developing states reveals that each 10-point increase in civil–military accountability yields a 0.4% rise in annual GDP growth.

Indonesia's transition demonstrates the synergy: after democratization, investment inflows grew from US $3 billion (1999) to US $45 billion (2023). Conversely, Egypt's military-led economy crowds out private investment; foreign direct investment fell 42% between 2018 and 2023 (Transparency International, 2024).

6.3.3 Political Stability

Between 1990 and 2025, the probability of coup attempts declined by 78% in countries adopting legal restraints on command authority. This suggests that *constitutional ethics* are a deterrent mechanism comparable to economic incentives.

Democracy survives when soldiers internalize a non-political identity. The OLAC model operationalizes this identity through law.

6.4 Global Policy Implications

6.4.1 International Law Reform

The international community, through the United Nations and regional organizations, can adopt binding conventions reinforcing lawful obedience.

A proposed UN Convention on Military Ethics and Lawful Command (UN-MELC) could mandate:

1.   Domestic constitutional clauses recognizing the right of lawful refusal.
2.   Training standards under UN peacekeeping certification.
3.   Periodic national reporting under Human Rights Council review.

This parallels the Convention against Torture (1984), converting moral aspiration into treaty obligation.

6.4.2 Role of Regional Blocs

- **ASEAN:** Indonesia could lead by drafting a *Jakarta Charter on Military Ethics*—a regional code emphasizing non-intervention and lawful obedience.
- **SAARC:** Pakistan, Bangladesh, and Nepal could collaborate on a *South Asian Charter of Civil–Military Ethics* coordinated with SAARC's Social Charter.
- **African Union:** Incorporate ethical command principles into the AU's Peace and Security Protocol, binding member states to investigate unlawful orders.
- **Organization of Islamic Cooperation (OIC):** Issue a collective *Fatwa of Justice* affirming that obedience in oppression is un-Islamic. This theological endorsement would neutralize extremist manipulation of obedience.

6.4.3 Global Education Networks

International military academies could form a Consortium of Ethical Command (CEC) linking Indonesia's Defense University, Pakistan's National Defence University, Nigeria's Defence Academy, and Chile's War College. Shared curricula, exchange programs, and simulation exercises would propagate lawful command as a professional standard rather than a Western import.

6.5 Ethical Command as a Development Paradigm

Traditional development theories emphasize capital accumulation and governance reform. Yet the comparative evidence here suggests that ethical command—the disciplined refusal to violate rights—is itself a developmental factor.

1. Governance quality: Ethical militaries reduce corruption by eliminating coercive rent-seeking.
2. Social trust: Citizens cooperate with lawful authorities, lowering transaction costs.

3.   Human capital: A professional, rights-respecting army retains skilled officers and attracts educated recruits.

4.   Gender inclusion: Ethical institutions are more likely to support female participation in armed services and public life.

Thus, constitutionalizing lawful refusal not only prevents abuse but actively accelerates modernization.

6.6 Toward a Global South Alliance of Reform

6.6.1 Shared Historical Burdens

Most post-colonial states inherited militaries designed for control, not representation. Whether under Dutch, British, French, or Ottoman rule, colonial militaries served governors, not citizens. The continuity of command culture explains why post-independence elites often replaced colonial masters without altering coercive logic.

6.6.2 Shared Reform Opportunities

Global South cooperation can break this cycle. An Alliance of Ethical Armed Forces (AEAF)—anchored by Indonesia, Pakistan, Nigeria, and Chile—could standardize training and monitoring protocols. Such cooperation would provide collective legitimacy for reform-minded officers facing domestic resistance.

6.6.3 Role of Technology and Data

Artificial intelligence and blockchain can enable transparent chain-of-command monitoring. Smart-order systems could log directives with digital signatures, allowing verification of legality and real-time oversight by constitutional auditors. Pilot programs in Indonesia's Ministry of Defense already test similar systems (2025 DefenseTech White Paper).

6.7 The Moral Economy of Obedience

Every military system embodies an implicit moral economy: what behavior is rewarded, punished, or honored. In authoritarian settings, obedience to command is rewarded even when illegal; conscience is punished as insubordination.

Lawful-refusal reform reverses this moral economy. It transforms courage from killing without question to questioning without fear.

Historical examples illustrate this transformation:

- In Chile, officers who refused Pinochet's late-stage repressive orders became national heroes.
- In Indonesia, student protests honored police and soldiers who refused violence during *Reformasi*.
- In Pakistan, public admiration for officers aiding civilians in disaster zones demonstrates the latent moral expectation for ethical service.

Embedding such recognition into official honors systems—*Medal for Lawful Valor, Award for Constitutional Duty*—will institutionalize conscience as valor.

6.8 Anticipating the Future: Risks of Regression

Even reformed militaries can regress. The 2025 Indonesian Military Service Bill and Egypt's expanding military economy reveal that authoritarian reflexes survive under democratic façades.

To prevent regression, reform must evolve from episodic to systemic— embedded in culture, education, and oversight.

Key preventive strategies:

1. Automatic Review Clause: Every ten years, parliaments must review compliance with lawful-refusal standards.
2. Sunset Clauses: Any extraordinary military powers granted during emergencies automatically expire after 180 days.

3. Civic Education Continuity: Civilians must remain aware of their oversight rights.

4. International Peer Review: Regular evaluation by AEAF or UN-MELC networks sustains pressure for transparency.

6.9 Integrating the Doctrine into Global Human Rights Architecture

The OLAC doctrine bridges civil–military reform and human rights law. It expands the scope of individual rights to include soldiers as moral citizens. Just as the Universal Declaration of Human Rights (1948) redefined the relationship between state and citizen, OLAC redefines that between command and conscience.

Proposed addition to future Human Rights Treaties:

> *"No member of any security institution shall be compelled to execute an order manifestly contrary to fundamental human rights, and all states shall ensure the right to lawful refusal and protection from retaliation."*

Such a clause, once adopted, would elevate lawful refusal to the same normative status as freedom of speech or assembly.

6.10 Global Vision: From Discipline to Conscience

The ultimate lesson of comparative history is that discipline without conscience breeds cruelty, while conscience without structure breeds anarchy. The fusion of both—lawful conscience within disciplined structure—is the foundation of modern civilization.

In the 21st century, the challenge is not to abolish armies but to humanize them. Ethical militaries will be central to solving crises—from disaster response to peacekeeping—where force must coexist with compassion. The same hands that once suppressed dissent can rebuild nations if guided by legality.

A soldier who protects a citizen from unlawful command becomes a symbol of rebirth. When this principle governs not one nation but many, humanity itself will have transcended the cycle of tyranny.

6.11 Conclusion: A Universal Charter for Ethical Command

Across Indonesia, Pakistan, Egypt, Nigeria, and beyond, the path to reform converges on one truth: the law must govern even those who hold the gun. The proposed *Charter for Ethical Command and Lawful Obedience* offers a moral constitution for the military age. Its clauses of lawful refusal, self-defense, and constitutional allegiance provide a universal standard compatible with every culture and faith.

The transformation will not be easy. It requires courage from civilians to legislate, from soldiers to question, and from commanders to yield. Yet history shows that when moral clarity meets institutional design, even entrenched authoritarianism can be reversed.

The world's future stability depends not only on disarmament of weapons but on enlightenment of those who bear them. To obey the law above command is to place conscience at the heart of power—
and in doing so, to make power truly serve the people.

Final Vision

The starting point of this study was military ethics,
but its ultimate destination is human dignity.

The strength of a nation is no longer measured by the sum of its violence,
but by its capacity for self-restraint and moral discipline.

The loyalty of a soldier must no longer be defined as obedience to an individual,
but as a pledge to the constitution and to the people.

When that day comes—

when the youth of Lahore,
the cadets of Jakarta,
and the soldiers of Cairo
can stand upright and declare with pride:

    "My loyalty is not to the state itself,
    but to the law that governs the state."

    Then democracy will transcend institutions;
    it will become culture,
    and it will become soul.

    That moment will mark the true transformation of humanity—
from fear to trust,
from power to principle,
from violence to justice.

Section 7: Comparative Findings and Lessons for Reforming Transitional States

A comparative review of Indonesia, Pakistan, Egypt, Nigeria, Chile, Brazil, Myanmar, and Cambodia reveals a consistent pattern:

the sustainability of democracy depends on whether the military transforms from a "tool of rulers" into a "guardian of the constitution."

1. Institutional Lessons

Indonesia's experience demonstrates that militaries are not inherently anti-democratic. When the constitution clearly defines the legal boundaries of military authority, soldiers can become defenders of law rather than instruments of power. In contrast, Pakistan and Egypt—where civilian governments rely on the military for political stability—have failed to develop institutional competence.

→ Conclusion: Only when "obedience to law above command" is constitutionally enshrined can a genuine balance of power emerge.

2. Cultural Lessons

Cultural transformation within the armed forces is the slowest yet most decisive element of political reform. The cases of Chile and Germany show that ethical education, transparent accountability, and reconstructed honor systems can change a soldier's identity within a single generation.

→ Conclusion: The essence of military reform lies not in weapons, but in thought.

3. Economic Lessons

Detaching the military from business interests marks the turning point from power to responsibility. Indonesia's 2004 Defense Law banned military-owned enterprises, opening the way for civilian oversight; Egypt and Pakistan, however, remain dominated by "military–business complexes" that drain public resources.

→ Conclusion: When the military exits the market, the nation restores economic fairness.

4. Social Lessons

When the armed forces cease suppressing citizens and instead serve in disaster relief, education, and infrastructure, public trust rises dramatically. In Indonesia, the TNI's humanitarian work during national disasters restored pride in the uniform—offering Pakistan a replicable model.

→ Conclusion: Moral legitimacy, not coercive force, sustains the state.

Overall Finding:

Every successful reform follows three interlinked transformations:

(1) from command to law,

(2) from power to responsibility, and

(3) from fear to trust.

This structural transition is not merely institutional—it represents a civilizational renewal.

Section 8: Policy Recommendations and the Vision of a Global "Charter for Ethical Command"

1. Establishing International Norms

The United Nations should initiate a Convention on Military Ethics and Lawful Command (UN-MELC) requiring all member states to:

- Enshrine the right of lawful refusal in their constitutions;

- Integrate it into UN peacekeeping training;

- Report periodically under the Human Rights Council framework.

2. Regional Cooperation Mechanisms

- ASEAN: Indonesia could lead the creation of a Jakarta Charter on Military Ethics emphasizing "non-intervention but lawful obedience."

- SAARC: Pakistan, Bangladesh, and Nepal could form a South Asian Forum on Civil–Military Ethics.

- African Union: Integrate lawful obedience into the AU Peace and Security Protocol.

- Organization of Islamic Cooperation (OIC): Issue a collective Fatwa of Justice affirming that "obedience in oppression is un-Islamic."

3. National-Level Reform Pathways

- Constitutional Amendments: Redefine the soldier's supreme loyalty as belonging to the constitution and the people.

- Ethical Education: Make human rights, constitutional law, and religious ethics core military academy subjects.

- Economic Transparency: Gradually dismantle military-owned enterprises through parliamentary audits.

- Protection Mechanisms: Establish independent Military Ethics Commissions to protect those who refuse unlawful orders from retaliation.

4. International Research and Data Infrastructure

Create a Global Observatory for Military Ethics (GOME) to publish an annual Global Military Ethics Index, measuring each nation's compliance with lawful obedience and human-rights standards.

Epilogue: The Age of Ethical Command

In an era where technology amplifies the destructive power of violence, the moral compass of those who hold the gun becomes civilization's last line of defense.

To refuse an unlawful order is not merely a legal reform—it is humanity's safeguard against self-destruction.

When a soldier can say with conviction:

"I obey orders, but first I obey my conscience.
I protect the nation, but above all, I protect the law."

Then the state will no longer sustain order through fear,

but through trust and justice.

That is the future—

a world armed with conscience,

a civilization where the military protects humanity itself.

www.ingramcontent.com/pod-product-compliance
Lightning Source LLC
Chambersburg PA
CBHW081407270326
41931CB00016B/3406